S0-AGF-057

Lab Manual for
PSYCHOLOGICAL
RESEARCH

Revised 3rd Edition

SAGE was founded in 1965 by Sara Miller McCune to support the dissemination of usable knowledge by publishing innovative and high-quality research and teaching content. Today, we publish more than 850 journals, including those of more than 300 learned societies, more than 800 new books per year, and a growing range of library products including archives, data, case studies, reports, and video. SAGE remains majority-owned by our founder, and after Sara's lifetime will become owned by a charitable trust that secures our continued independence.

Los Angeles | London | New Delhi | Singapore | Washington DC

Lab Manual for
PSYCHOLOGICAL RESEARCH

Revised 3rd Edition

Dawn M. McBride
J. Cooper Cutting
Illinois State University

Los Angeles | London | New Delhi
Singapore | Washington DC

Los Angeles | London | New Delhi
Singapore | Washington DC

FOR INFORMATION:

SAGE Publications, Inc.
2455 Teller Road
Thousand Oaks, California 91320
E-mail: order@sagepub.com

SAGE Publications Ltd.
1 Oliver's Yard
55 City Road
London EC1Y 1SP
United Kingdom

SAGE Publications India Pvt. Ltd.
B 1/I 1 Mohan Cooperative Industrial Area
Mathura Road, New Delhi 110 044
India

SAGE Publications Asia-Pacific Pte. Ltd.
3 Church Street
#10-04 Samsung Hub
Singapore 049483

Copyright © 2016 by SAGE Publications, Inc.

All rights reserved. No part of this book may be reproduced or utilized in any form or by any means, electronic or mechanical, including photocopying, recording, or by any information storage and retrieval system, without permission in writing from the publisher.

Printed in the United States of America

Library of Congress Cataloging-in-Publication Data

McBride, Dawn M.

Lab manual for psychological research / Dawn M. McBride and J. Cooper Cutting. — Revised 3rd edition.

pages cm
Includes bibliographical references and index.

ISBN 978-1-5063-1134-0 (pbk. : alk. paper) 1. Psychology—Research—Methodology. I. Cutting, J. Cooper. II. Title.

BF76.5.M375 2016
150.72'4—dc23   2015022793

This book is printed on acid-free paper.

SFI label applies to text stock

Acquisitions Editor: Reid Hester
Associate Editor: Nathan Davidson
Editorial Assistant: Morgan McCardell
Production Editor: Jane Haenel
Copy Editor: Kristin Bergstad
Typesetter: C&M Digitals (P) Ltd.
Proofreader: Tricia Currie-Knight
Indexer: Terri Corry
Cover Designer: Candice Harman
Marketing Manager: Shari Countryman

17 18 19 20 21 10 9 8 7 6 5 4 3 2

Contents

Introduction for Instructors

The *Lab Manual for Psychological Research* is designed to allow instructors to choose from assignments that give students practice with knowledge and skills learned in a research methods course. The manual contains four major components: (1) exercises that connect to specific concepts in the course, (2) exercises geared toward the development of a research project, (3) APA style exercises that become progressively more complex, and (4) instruction on how to avoid plagiarism. The intent is to provide exercises on various aspects of a methods course that instructors may choose to assign to students. Assignments that instructors choose not to include as required can provide students with study aids for the concepts covered. A solution key is posted on the instructor website at **edge.sagepub.com/mcbride3e.** Exercises in the first component cover major course concepts such as design types and observation techniques, literature reviews and library research, reading journal articles, identifying variables, ethical guidelines, subject sampling, and descriptive and inferential statistics. Learning checks are included that could serve as quizzes for topics covered in this section of the manual.

In the second component, a research development project is included that can be assigned to groups or individuals and completed throughout the course as students learn the steps in designing research studies. This component includes assignments related to choosing a research topic, conducting a literature review, developing a method, analyzing and interpreting results, and presenting the project as an oral or poster presentation. These assignments progress through the topics in the course and thus can be assigned at different points in the course after different topics have been covered that allow students to continue in their development of the project.

The third component includes APA style exercises that begin with simple APA guidelines and progress to evaluation of short articles for APA style violations.

Finally, the manual includes explanations of and exercises on plagiarism to help students understand what is and isn't plagiarism and how to avoid it in their writing.

New to this edition: 13 new exercises were added to this edition to provide more options for instructors to help students develop more difficult skills in the course. These include:

- 2 new Factorials Design exercises
- 3 new Journal Article exercises
- Correlations and Scatterplots Exercise
- Experiments Exercise
- Design and Data Collection Exercise
- Identifying and Developing Hypotheses About Variables Exercise
- Inferential Statistics and Analysis Exercise
- Internal and External Validity Exercise
- Design a Study Exercise
- Specialized Designs Exercise: Developmental

Acknowledgments

T he authors would like to acknowledge the contributions of several important people to materials in this lab manual. Improvement of the lab assignments was made from feedback given by our past graduate student teaching assistants Allison Bock, Jim Clinton, Jennifer Coane, Charles Coey, Angela Conte, F. Andy Eichler, Adam Hampton, Tanya Henderson, Derek Herrmann, Amanda Kearney, Katy Melcher, Andrew Monroe, Ryan Seltzer, Diana Steakley-Freeman, and Chris Wahlheim. We also thank the helpful folks at SAGE. Finally, we thank our past PSY 231 students at Illinois State University for providing inspiration for the assignments in this manual.

The authors and SAGE would like to acknowledge the contributions of the following reviewers:

Andrea Friedrich, *University of Kentucky*

Asiye Kumru, *Ozyegin University*

Vanessa Miller, *Texas Christian University*

Charlsie Myers, *College of Coastal Georgia*

Shawn Powell, *Casper College*

Allison Pulizzi, *SUNY College at Old Westbury*

Ron Salazar, *San Juan College*

Adam Shavit, *The City University of New York*

L. James Smart, *Miami University (Ohio)*

Grace White, *University of Central Florida*

PART I

Research Methods Exercises

Exercises in the first component cover major course concepts such as design types and observation techniques, literature reviews and library research, reading journal articles, identifying variables, ethical guidelines, subject sampling, and descriptive and inferential statistics.

1. Knowledge Exercise: What Do We Know and How Do We Know It?

1. Write down four things that you know. Then, for each, write down how you know these things. Categorize your ways of knowing (i.e., intuition, authority, or observation).

   a.

   b.

   c.

   d.

2. Think of a piece of knowledge that you acquired using the method of:

   Intuition:

   Authority:

   Observation:

2. Science Versus Pseudoscience Exercise

One of the goals of the course you are taking is to help you recognize the difference between scientific evidence and pseudoscience. Knowledge gained with the scientific method relies on carefully controlled studies that produce results that can be replicated. In addition, according to Lawson (2007), there are six common characteristics of pseudoscience:

- Use of imprecise, scientific-sounding language
- No evidence of continued research or new knowledge gained over time
- Reliance on anecdotes as evidence
- Reliance on authority endorsements, especially "false authorities" (i.e., people who claim to be authorities but do not have any real expertise in the area)
- Extraordinary claims without supporting evidence
- Evidence relies on confirmation rather than refutation

There are many advertisements presented in the media (e.g., TV commercials, newspaper and magazine ads) that rely on pseudoscience to advertise a claim or product. For this exercise, find such an advertisement and write a short paragraph that (1) describes the claim or product, (2) identifies any of the above elements of pseudoscience used in the ad, and (3) explains why the ad relies more on pseudoscience than science for its claims.

3. Design a Study Exercise

Design a research study to answer one of the research questions below. Then answer the questions that follow about the study you designed.

- Choose a research question:

  1. Does exposure to violence cause someone to be more violent?
  2. Does having more money mean you are happier?
  3. Does consumption of caffeine increase work productivity?

- Consider what behavior(s) will be observed, how you can rule out alternative explanations of results, and how your observations can answer the question.

  1. Which research question did you choose?

  2. What are the operational definitions in your study?

  3. What behavior(s) that you observe will answer the research question (i.e., how will you know the answer from the behaviors you are observing)?

  4. What are some alternative explanations of those behaviors (other than the factor listed in the research question)?

4. Naturalistic Observation Group Exercise

Research Questions

1. Do people walking alone walk faster than people walking in groups of two or more?

2. Which campus building has more traffic (i.e., people going in and out) between classes?

3. Do more males or females hang out on the quad between classes?

4. Which entrance to the Student Center is used most often between classes?

Research Procedures

1. As a group, discuss your research question and decide on a reasonable predicted answer to your research question. Be sure to record WHY you think this is the answer you will obtain.

2. As a group, discuss ways to use naturalistic observation of people on campus to answer your research question. Be sure to decide on the following:

   a. How long you will observe your subjects (no longer than 20 minutes)

   b. How you will observe the subjects UNOBTRUSIVELY

   c. What you will observe/measure

   d. How your observations will answer your research question (i.e., what observations do you expect if your prediction is correct?)

   e. Identify your independent/subject variable and your dependent variable(s)

3. Conduct your study and collect your observations.

4. Discuss what you found in your observations and how you would answer your research question based on those observations.

5. Prepare and present to the class:

   a. Your research question and prediction (including why you made that prediction)

   b. Your variables (identify whether you have an independent or subject variable and your dependent variable)

   c. Your method (how you obtained your observations)

   d. The answer to your research question from your observations

   e. Any limitations you found using this method to answer your question

6. Briefly discuss what worked well and what didn't work well with your naturalistic observation. If you had it to do all over again, what would you do differently? Why?

5. Survey Research Exercise

Constructs

A. Friendliness

B. Introversion

C. Helpfulness

D. Depression

E. Intelligence

F. Punctuality

G. Flexibility

H. Anxiety

Instructions

1. As a group, discuss your construct and some behaviors that might tell you how a person rates on the construct.

2. Decide on a measurement scale. Use closed-ended questions. Decide what categories you will use as responses. If you are using a Likert scale, be sure to define the range of responses and include anchors. Also discuss a way you might verify the reliability of your survey.

3. Write 10 items for your survey that assess your construct. Be sure to write questions as clearly as possible and using simple language. Be sure each member of your group has a copy of the complete survey with exact wording.

4. Administer your survey to someone you think is high on the construct and to someone you think is low on the construct. Compare their responses to your predictions about them.

5. Prepare to present to the class (in your group) at the next class meeting:

   a. Your construct and some behaviors your group thought were related to the construct

   b. A sample copy of the survey

   c. A summary of the responses you got and how well the responses matched your predictions about the people

   d. An overall evaluation of the validity of your survey

   e. A method for testing the reliability of your survey

6. Elect someone from your group to present the information in (5) with the help of others in the group.

6. Science in the News

Find an article in the newspaper that reports the results of some research (Hint: check the science section). For that article, try to identify as many "scientific method details" about the research as you can.

For example: What was the hypothesis for the research? What methodology was used (e.g., experimental, correlational, case study)? How were the participants obtained? What were the conclusions of the research? What were the limitations of the study?

How convinced are you by the study's results? What questions about the research do you have? What other details were left out that would be useful in evaluating the quality of the study?

7. How to Read Empirical Journal Articles

Published journal articles in psychology have a particular format that allows readers to find the information they are looking for and makes the study report clearer to the readers. Most articles will follow APA (American Psychological Association) style guidelines, organizing the paper into the following major sections:

- Abstract
- Introduction
- Method
- Results
- Discussion
- References

We'll discuss each of the sections to familiarize you with the information you can expect to find in these sections.

Abstract

An Abstract is a concise summary of the study that includes the purpose, method, main results, and conclusions of the study. The Abstract must be short (under 120 words for APA style), because the Abstract will be entered into the PsycINFO database to provide researchers with enough information to decide if the article is relevant to their interests. The Abstract is usually the first (and possibly the only) portion of the article that a reader will encounter. It is printed at the top of the first page of the article.

Introduction

The Introduction contains a lot of important information about the background and motivation for the study. A well-written Introduction will begin by introducing the general topic of the study (i.e., the research question) and defining any specialized terms. The author(s) will then review what is already known about the research question by discussing past studies conducted in the area, the results found, and the relevance of each study to the current study described in the article. The author(s) will also describe the purpose/motivation for the current study, explaining why it was done and how the design used allowed them to answer the research question. In most cases, hypotheses will also be stated according to the specific results that were expected for the study.

A well-written Introduction will make a clear argument for why the study is important. A reader should be able to find the argument for the study's purpose and the support provided by the author(s) in the form of a research question that has not yet been fully addressed by past studies in the topic area.

Method

The Method section is a detailed description of the design and methodology of the study. It is divided into four main subsections: Participants, Design, Materials or Apparatus, and Procedure. Some articles may combine some of these subsections into a single section (e.g., Design and Materials as one section). The goal of the Method section is to allow someone to replicate the important elements of the study if they wish to do so.

Participants: This section describes the important characteristics of the participants in the study. The information should include the number of participants, important demographic information, number of participants per condition, where participants were sampled from, and compensation provided for the participants.

Design: If a separate Design section is included, it will describe the variables that were manipulated and/or measured in the study. If the study is an experiment, level of the independent variables will be described and how the variables were manipulated will also be included (e.g., within-subjects, between-subjects).

Materials or Apparatus: The Materials or Apparatus section will describe the relevant materials or apparatus used for the study. Examples include specialized apparatus used for the study, computers used to present stimuli or collect responses, stimuli presented to the participants and how they were developed, questionnaires given to participants and relevant information about them, and so on. Sometimes the actual items used will be presented in an Appendix that is referred to in the Materials section.

Procedure: The Procedure section should provide a chronological ordering of what the participants experienced during the study, including instructions for the tasks, what they saw or read, timing of presentation or task completion, what task they performed, what responses were collected from them, different conditions of the study and how participants were assigned to the conditions, and so on.

Results

The Results section will include an objective report of the results found in the study. This section should include a description of the data collected and the statistical tests used to analyze the data. Summary information about the data will also be included either within the text or in Tables/Graphs that are referred to in the Results section. Statistical test results and values will also be included in the text.

Discussion

The Discussion section should review hypotheses (if they were stated in the Introduction) and discuss the results in reference to the original research question. It should be clear from the Discussion section what answer to the research question was provided by the study. A comparison with results of past studies will also be included and possible explanations for discrepant or unexpected results should be provided by the author(s). The author(s) may also suggest directions for future studies in the topic area.

References

Every past study cited in the paper should be included in the References section of the article in alphabetical order. If you are researching studies in a particular area, the References section can be useful in providing leads to other relevant articles in a particular topic area. Each reference will include the authors' last names and initials in the order of authorship on the paper (this order is important—it usually indicates the order of contribution to the published article), the year the article was published, the title of the article, the journal it was published in, and the volume and page numbers of the journal.

Multiple Study/Experiment Articles

Many articles published in psychology contain more than one study or experiment. For those articles, you are likely to see a separate Method and Results section for each article, but just one Introduction and one General Discussion section that tie the whole article together.

8. Reading Journal Articles Exercise—Assefi and Garry (2003)

This exercise accompanies a reading of:

Assefi, S. L., & Garry, M. (2003). Absolut memory distortions: Alcohol placebos influence the misinformation effect. *Psychological Science, 14,* 77–80.

Please answer the following questions about the Assefi and Garry article (you must read through the article before you begin this assignment—the reference to the article is provided above and can be found on the Sage Student Site). For each question, indicate which section of the article (e.g., Introduction, Method) the information was in.

1. What is the research question?

2. How did they answer the research question? (Hint: you should be able to answer this question by reading the Introduction of the article.)

3. Do the authors make a hypothesis? If so, what is it?

4. What type of research design (e.g., correlational study, experiment, quasi-experiment) did the authors use?

5. Do you think the data collection technique used in the study qualifies as naturalistic observation? Why or why not?

6. What was measured in the study and *how* was it measured? (Hint: Two things were measured—see the headings in the Results and Discussion sections.)

7. How was the influence of alcohol examined in this study? (Hint: Read the Method section carefully.)

8. What was the difference between the "control items" and the "misled items"?

9. What do the results shown in Figure 1 tell you about how social factors affect memory performance?

10. How did the "told alcohol" condition affect the subjects' confidence in their memories?

11. Based on the results, what answer did the authors get to their research question?

12. What is the main piece of information learned by this study?

13. Based on what was learned, what real-world application does this study have?

9. Reading Journal Articles
Exercise—Mueller and Oppenheimer (2014)

This exercise accompanies a reading of:

Mueller, P. A., & Oppenheimer, D. M. (2014). The pen is mightier than the keyboard: Advantages of longhand over laptop notetaking. *Psychological Science, 25,* 1159–1168.

Please answer the following questions about the Mueller and Oppenheimer article (you must read through the article before you begin this assignment—the reference to the article is provided above and can be found on the Sage Student Site). For each question, indicate which section of the article (e.g., Introduction, Method) the information was in.

1. State the research question.

2. Discuss some of the past research regarding hand note taking versus laptop note taking. Which is more advantageous to learning? (Hint: all researchers may not agree.)

3. Do the researchers state a specific hypothesis? If so, what is it? If not, what is your hypothesis (or prediction)?

4. Study 1: How did the researchers design the experiment to answer their research question? (This can be found in the Method section.)

5. What change in methodology did the researchers make from Study 1 to Study 2? Why?

6. Was the above change effective in answering their follow-up question?

7. What were some possible limitations of Study 2, and how did they design Study 3 to alleviate those limitations?

8. Briefly summarize the main (and important) findings from Study 1, Study 2, and Study 3.

9. Overall, what do the results suggest for note taking?

10. What are some real-world applications of this study, and how can students use this information for their own learning?

10. Reading Journal Articles Exercise— Lee et al. (2014)

This exercise accompanies a reading of:

Lee, K., Talwar, V., McCarthy, A., Ross, I., Evans, A., & Arruda, C. (2014). Can classic moral stories promote honesty in children? *Psychological Science, 25,* 1630–1636.

Please answer the following questions about the Lee et al. article (you must read through the article before you begin this assignment—the reference to the article is provided above and can be found on the Sage Student Site). For each question, indicate which section of the article (e.g., Introduction, Method) the information was in.

1. Explain why, specifically, the three stories utilized in Experiment 1 were chosen as modes of researching honesty in children for this experiment. How do these stories differ from each other in a way that can be accurately tested?

2. Explain the modified temptation-resistance task used in this experiment. Do you think this is a good task for measuring lying in children? Why or why not?

3. What were the hypotheses for the three stories presented? Be sure to differentiate these predictions between the younger and older children.

4. Explain the purpose behind why "The Tortoise and the Hare" was used in this experiment.

5. The children in Experiment 1 were coded into three separate groups. What were these, and how was this coding procedure conducted?

6. Based on the results from Experiment 1, what answer did the authors get to their research question?

7. What was added for Experiment 2, and what was the purpose of adding this factor?

8. Utilizing the results presented in Table 1 and Figure 1, answer the following questions:

   a. How common was peeking behavior?

   b. What variable was a significant predictor of peeking behavior in children?

   c. What variable was a significant predictor of honesty in children who did peek?

9. What did the results from the manipulation in Experiment 2 tell us about lying and honesty in children?

10. It is noted when discussing the limitations of the study that the researchers told the children to emulate the protagonist of each story. What sort of confound does this create in the results? What are some potential ways in which this could be changed to eliminate this confound?

11. How does the information you learned in this article relate to previous concepts you may have learned in other psychology courses (e.g., positive reinforcement, positive punishment, negative reinforcement, negative punishment, classical conditioning, etc.)?

12. The stories used in these experiments are models that represented the immediate negative effects of lying (Pinocchio/Negative George Washington), the delayed negative effects of lying (The Boy Who Cried Wolf), and the immediate positive effects of honesty (George Washington and the Cherry Tree). What might you predict the results to be if a story was included about the *delayed positive effects* of honesty? Why?

13. Do you think influence from media (childhood movies, television shows, etc.), instead of childhood picture books, might be any more effective in promoting honesty? Why?

14. Is it possible to apply the results from this study to ages past childhood? For instance, if one were attempting to investigate how to promote honesty and reduce lying behavior in adolescents, how could this study be modified?

15. How might the results from this study apply to other moral conventions that we attempt to teach children (e.g., manners, bullying, hard work)? In what ways might the study have to be modified to investigate other moral conventions?

11. Reading Journal Articles
Exercise—Roediger and Karpicke (2006)

This exercise accompanies a reading of:

Roediger, H. L., III, Karpicke, J. D. (2006). Test-enhanced learning: Taking memory tests improves long-term retention. *Psychological Science, 17,* 249–255.

Please answer the following questions about the Roediger and Karpicke article (you must read through the article before you begin this assignment—the reference to the article is provided above and can be found on the Sage Student Site).

1. The research question addressed in this study is
   a. Of all study techniques, which is the best?
   b. Which study technique do students use most often?
   c. Which study technique is better: re-reading or recalling?
   d. Which information is better remembered: a story about otters or a story about the sun?

2. The researchers' hypothesis in this study is
   a. Information about otters will be remembered better than information about the sun.
   b. Recalling information will result in better memory than re-reading the information.
   c. Re-reading information will result in better memory than recalling information.
   d. None of the above.

3. Learning condition in Experiment 1 was manipulated within-subjects. This means that
   a. all subjects received both the re-reading and recalling learning conditions.
   b. subjects only completed either the re-reading or the recalling learning condition.
   c. subjects did not receive either of these conditions in the study.

4. The main results of Experiment 1 were that
   a. recall for the otter passage was higher than recall for the sun passage.
   b. recall was higher when subjects recalled the passage than when they re-read the passage before the final test for all test delays.
   c. subjects recalled more about the passage they found more interesting.
   d. recall was higher when subjects recalled the passage than when they re-read the passage before the final test, but only for test delays greater than 5 min.

5. Experiment 2 as conducted to
   a. replicate the results of Experiment 1.
   b. generalize the results of Experiment 1 to new passages.
   c. Examine effects of taking multiple tests between study and the final test.
   d. Both a and c.

6. The results of Experiment 2 showed that
   a. recalling the passages always resulted in better memory than re-reading them.

    b. repeated tests of the passages resulted in less forgetting over the 1 week delay than the other learning conditions.

    c. subjects recalled less information when the passages were changed.

7. The primary conclusion from this study is that
    a. people remember more about animals than other topics.
    b. recalling information will help you remember better than re-reading it over the long term.
    c. the best study technique for students seems to be re-reading their notes.
    d. all of the above.

12. Lab Assignment: Library Exercise

1. How does an empirical journal article differ from a popular magazine article (e.g., an article in *Time* magazine)? Who is the intended audience of empirical journal articles in psychology?

2. Describe how you might use PsycINFO to conduct a literature review on the topic of **obesity stereotypes and biases.** Describe the steps you would take to collect relevant articles for your literature review and what you might expect to find at each step.

3. Using PsycINFO, find an article authored by Larry L. Jacoby that was published in 1991 and then write the APA style reference for the article below.

4. Using PsycINFO, find a **recent article (2005–2012)** that examines the relationship between violence on TV and violent behavior in children. Write the APA style reference for the article below.

5. You've probably heard the saying "Opposites attract." This is really a hypothesis about what people are attracted to, and research in psychology has attempted to test this hypothesis. For this exercise, you will search for studies that tested this hypothesis. However, before you begin, you must first convert the saying into a research question about behavior.

a. State the research question for this saying in terms of behavior that might be examined in a research study.

b. Using your research question to develop keywords (do NOT type in the saying), conduct a literature search using PsycINFO to find one article that provides empirical evidence that either supports or does not support the hypothesis. In your own words, write a paragraph indicating why you think the article supports or does not support the hypothesis. Attach a copy of the Abstract of the article and describe how you conducted your search.

c. Describe how the empirical evidence you found could be used by companies that run dating sites (e.g., match.com) to help their clients identify potential dating partners.

13. Learning Check—Basics of Psychological Research

Short-Answer Questions

1. Give an operational definition for "hungry."

2. Give an example of a hypothesis that can be made from the theory "sleeplessness causes depression."

3. What is the difference between a data-driven hypothesis and a theory-driven hypothesis?

4. What is the purpose of conducting a literature review when conducting a research study?

5. In what ways does naturalistic observation differ from other data collection techniques?

Multiple-Choice Questions

6. Psychologists use which method of knowing in learning about behavior?

   a. logic
   b. authority
   c. observation
   d. intuition

7. Which of the following is NOT a key element of an experiment?

   a. control
   b. an independent variable
   c. naturalistic observation
   d. causal explanations

8. The best synonym for a theory is

   a. a prediction.

   b. an explanation.

   c. a bias.

   d. an independent variable.

A study was conducted to learn about the social interactions of elementary-aged schoolchildren. The children were observed during recess for a 6-month time period. Results showed that as age of the children increased, they were more likely to have verbal interactions with their peers.

9. The study described above is an example of the _____ research method.

   a. experimental

   b. naturalistic

   c. case study

   d. correlational

10. The study described above employs the use of which data collection method?

    a. archival data

    b. naturalistic observation

    c. experimental data

    d. interviews

11. Which of the following was a dependent variable in the above study?

    a. age

    b. observation time

    c. social interaction

    d. a and c

    e. b and c

    f. none of the above

12. In which section of a journal article would you find a listing of the raw data?

    a. Introduction

    b. Method

    c. Results

    d. none of the above

14. Research Design Exercise

For the research questions below, design a study to answer the question using the research design specified. Be sure to describe any variables you would include in the study, as well as any operational definitions needed.

1. Does watching violence on TV cause violent behavior? (experiment)

2. Do people who play video games have better hand–eye coordination in other tasks? (correlational)

3. Does divorce in families negatively affect children? (case study)

4. Are smoking and lung cancer related? (quasi-experiment)

5. Does studying with background music improve test scores? (experiment)

6. Are there fewer helping behaviors in large cities? (correlational)

7. Are color and mood related? (correlational)

8. Are caffeine and work productivity related? (quasi-experiment)

9. Does watching violence on TV cause violent behavior? (correlational)

10. Do people who play video games have better hand–eye coordination in other tasks? (experiment)

15. Design and Data Collection Exercise

For each study description below, identify the data collection technique and the research design that were used.

1. Researchers (Bartecchi et al., 2006) were interested in the effects of a new law banning smoking in public places on health. They compared heart attack rates for two cities of comparable size where one city had enacted a smoking ban one year before the study and the other city had no smoking ban. To compare heart attack rates, the researchers examine hospital records for the hospitals in each city. They compared heart attacks rates for the year before the smoking ban in each city and for the year after the ban was enacted. They found that heart attack rates decreased in the city with the ban from one year to the next, but did not decrease in the city without the ban.

Data collection technique:

Research design:

2. To evaluate the validity of a newly created survey measure of college students' satisfaction with their major, a researcher (Nauta, 2007) administered the survey to college students who had declared a major. She then also collected the students' GPAs (with their permission) from the university registrar to examine the relationship between their survey score and their GPA. She found that satisfaction with major was positively correlated with GPA.

Data collection techniques (there is more than one in this study):

Research design:

What does it mean that she found a positive relationship between GPA and survey score?

3. Researchers (Assefi & Garry, 2003) were interested in the effects of the belief that one has consumed alcohol on cognition. In particular, they tested whether a belief that subjects had consumed alcohol during the study would increase their susceptibility to memory errors. Subjects were randomly assigned to one of two groups. In one group they were told the drink they consumed had contained alcohol (with some alcohol rubbed on the outside of the glass for realism). In the other group, they were told the drink did not contain alcohol. All subjects then saw a slide show of a crime (shoplifting). After a short delay, subjects then read a description of the crime that contained errors. After another short delay, they answered questions about the slides they had seen and were asked to rate their confidence in their answers. Subjects told they drank alcohol made more errors in their answers and were more confident in their responses.

Data collection technique:

Research design:

16. Identifying and Developing Hypotheses About Variables

Finding and developing research ideas takes practice. One source of some research ideas is our common wisdom. This exercise has you practice developing commonly held beliefs into testable research ideas. Listed below are 10 statements that are common pieces of cliché advice (many of which you may have heard at some point in your life). Pick two of the clichés, and turn them into testable research ideas.

Absence makes the heart grow fonder.	Experience is the best teacher.
All work and no play make Jack a very dull boy.	An apple never falls far from the tree.
Good fences make good neighbors.	He who laughs last, laughs longest.
Ignorance is bliss.	A rose by any other name still smells as sweet.
Opposites attract (relationships).	An apple a day keeps the doctor away.

For each of the clichés that you select:

- Identify a potential research method that may be used to investigate the idea.
- Identify the relevant variables and specify how the researcher might manipulate and/or measure the variables.
- Identify other variables that might be relevant (e.g., to control or measure).

Example: Laughter is the best medicine.

Research Method: Experiment

Independent Variable: "Laughter"
This variable may be operationalized by manipulating whether there is laughter present or absent.

Dependent Variables: "Best Medicine"— this probably could refer to many different variables that we consider "health."
This variable may be operationalized by measuring a variety of aspects of health:

- Physiological health may be measured with a standard physical examination by a physician.
- Psychological health may be measured with a set of questionnaires designed to measure aspects of psychological health.

Other potentially relevant variables: "Medicine" suggests that "laughter" is a treatment for an ailment, so factors like the type and severity of the ailment might be important variables to measure or control.

Cliché #1:

Cliché #2:

17. Experiments Exercise

Part 1: Imagine that you were a participant in an experiment where you were asked to eat cookies and rate how much you liked each cookie on a scale from 1 to 5, where higher ratings mean higher liking of the cookie. You are asked to eat an Oreo cookie and rate it and then eat a Chips Ahoy cookie and rate it. For this experiment, answer the questions below.

1. What is the independent variable (IV)? What are the levels of the IV?

2. Was the IV manipulated between-subjects or within-subjects? How do you know?

3. What is the dependent variable (DV)? What operational definition was used in this experiment?

4. What scale of measurement was used for the DV?

5. The IV was bivalent. Explain how you can make it multivalent.

6. Change the cookie experiment into a factorial experiment. Explain what you would need to add and what conditions you would have in your factorial experiment.

7. Do you think the cookie experiment has more internal validity or external validity? Explain your answer.

Part 2: Testing causal relationships—Roediger and Karpicke (2006):

One question students often ask is how they can best prepare for exams in their classes. This is a question that we can answer based on experiments. For example, some researchers (e.g., Roediger & Karpicke, 2006) wanted to know if "reading over your notes" is an effective way to remember information for a test. But they wanted to test the causal link between study method and memory so they compared two learning conditions for text material (e.g., a passage about sea otters) in an experiment to see which of the study conditions resulted in better memory performance. In one condition, subjects read through the passage and then tried to recall what they read without re-reading it. In the other condition, subjects read through the passage and then re-read the passage a few times for the same amount of time that the other group spent recalling the passage. Thus, this study compared techniques like "reading over your notes" or "re-reading chapters" that are reported fairly often with techniques like "quiz myself" and "teach to someone else" that are reported less frequently (see the graph on the next page for some sample data that students might report when asked what study techniques they use in preparing for exams). Both groups of subjects in the study took a final recall test on the passage after a delay. They found that after 2 days (let's pretend you all study for an exam 2 days before it instead of the night before), the read-test group recalled almost 70% of the passage ideas and the read-read group recalled only about 52% of the passage ideas. Use this study description to answer the questions below.

8. What is the independent variable in the Roediger and Karpicke (2006) study? What are the levels? How does this IV connect with real-world situations?

9. What was their dependent variable? How was it operationally defined?

10. Why does the Roediger and Karpicke (2006) study show that the read-test study technique *causes* one to remember better? Why don't the sample survey data below show that the "read over your notes" technique listed most often *causes* better test scores?

Sample data from class survey on study techniques:

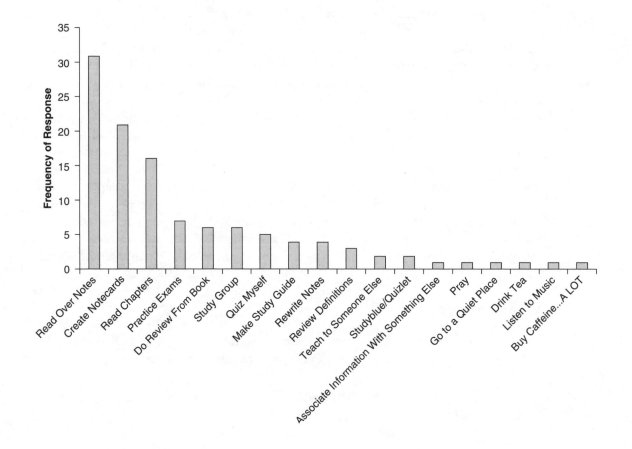

18. Independent and Dependent Variables Exercise

Part 1. Identifying Independent Variables (IV) and Dependent Variables (DV)

Remember that an independent variable is manipulated, while a dependent variable is measured and may change as a result of exposure to the independent variable.

1. Jury decisions are influenced by the attractiveness of the defendant.

    IV:

    DV:

2. A drug company is advertising a new drug that helps people recover from jet lag faster. You are skeptical, so you conduct an experiment to test their claim. In your experiment, 100 people are flown from San Francisco to Tokyo. During the flight, half the participants are given the drug company's new drug. The other half of the participants are given a placebo (i.e., sugar pill) during the flight. Six hours after they land, all participants are asked to rate how sleepy and disoriented they feel.

    IV:

    DV:

3. Vohs and Schooler (2008) conducted a study to investigate the effect of beliefs about free will on behavior. Thirty college students participated in their study. Participants were randomly assigned to read one of two paragraphs taken from the same book. One of the paragraphs suggested that scientists believe that free will is an illusion. The other paragraph discussed consciousness and did not mention the topic of free will. All participants were then asked to complete a set of math problems, presented one at a time on a computer screen. Participants were asked to complete each problem. They were also told that the computer program had an error such that the answers to some of the problems may appear with the problem and that they should try to solve the problems on their own (they could make the answer disappear by pressing the space bar when the problem appeared). The researchers measured the number of times the participants pressed the space bar as a measure of cheating behavior (more presses means less cheating).

IV:

DV:

Part 2. Operationally Defining Variables

Remember that the variables that we make hypotheses about are often abstract constructs. Designing research to examine the relationships between variables involves the process of operationally defining those variables in terms of how they are manipulated or measured. Consider each of the following research descriptions, identify the variables, and briefly describe how they are operationally defined.

4. The nonconscious mimicry of the behaviors of interacting partners is referred to as the chameleon effect. Chartrand and Bargh (1999) performed a study to examine how mimicry within an interaction influenced the quality of the interaction and liking between partners. They had pairs of participants describe what they saw in photographs. One of the participants in each pair was a confederate (working with the researchers). Half of the confederates were instructed to mirror the behaviors of their partner, while the other half engaged in neutral mannerisms. Following the picture description interaction, participants completed questionnaires asking them to report how much they liked their partner (the confederate) and how smoothly the interaction had gone. The results showed that participants rated the interaction smoother and reported liking their partners more in the mimic condition than in the neutral condition.

5. These days, advertising is a nearly omnipresent part of our lives. While we may be consciously aware of the obvious attempts of advertisers to influence our behaviors, we may not be aware of more subtle effects. Braun and Loftus (1998) conducted research in which they investigated how memories about an object (already experienced) can change as a function of advertising (presented after experiencing the object). In their first experiment, the researchers demonstrated that memories can be altered by presentation of misleading information in advertisements. Their follow-up experiment examined whether this effect would persist if people knew that the advertisements may contain misleading information. In this study, participants believed that they were participating in a chocolate taste test experiment. They were presented samples of the candy in a green wrapper, and they tasted and rated the product. Following a brief filler task, respondents were asked to evaluate advertisements for the product. The advertisement presented misleading information about the color of the wrapper (suggesting that the wrapper was blue). Following another brief filler task, participants were given a memory test for the color of the wrapper used in the taste test by selecting the color from a color wheel. The researchers also told the participants that some of the colors in the advertisement were not representative of the true colors. Some participants were told this when they saw the advertisements; others were told only at the memory test. The researchers again found a strong misinformation effect of the advertisement despite the explicit warnings given to participants. The effect was strongest when the warning was given at the memory test. The authors concluded that warning consumers about past misleading advertising may have little effect because the misinformation may have already become incorporated into memory.

19. Identifying Variables From Abstracts

1. Find the abstract for each of the following articles (either in PsycINFO or in the journal):

   - Logan, G. D. (2004) in *Journal of Experimental Psychology: General*
   - Ferreira, V. S., & Humphreys, K. R. (2001) in *Journal of Memory and Language*
   - Jordan, J. S., & Knoblich, G. (2004) in *Psychonomic Bulletin & Review*

2. Include a copy of these abstracts with your lab exercise.

3. Try to identify as many of the following as possible based on the abstract:

   a. who were the participants (e.g., kids, college students)

   b. independent and dependent variables

   c. main results

   d. implications of the results

20. Identifying Variables From Empirical Articles

This exercise accompanies a reading of Sayette, M. A., Reichle, E. D., & Schooler, J. W. (2009). Lost in the sauce: The effects of alcohol on mind wandering. *Psychological Science, 20,* 747–752.

Please answer the following questions about the variables used in the Sayette et al. study (you will need to read the article to answer most of the questions—the reference to the article is provided above and can be found on the SAGE Student Site).

1. The purpose of the Sayette et al. (2009) study was to investigate the effect of alcohol on mind wandering (i.e., lapses of attention to a task). Based on the purpose and title of the article (and without reading the article), what do you think the independent and dependent variables in this study were?

   IV:

   DV:

2. After reading the article, can you state the authors' research question using the conditions in their study?

3. What was the primary independent variable in the study? How was it manipulated (i.e., what was the researchers' operational definition of "alcohol")?

4. What were the dependent variables in the study (i.e., how did the researchers operationally define "mind wandering")? How were they measured?

5. What results were found in a comparison of the independent variable groups for each dependent variable? In other words, for which dependent variables were there group differences and which group had a higher mean score on each dependent variable?

6. Overall, what did the authors learn from this study?

21. Internal and External Validity Exercise

For each Abstract below, evaluate the internal and external validity of the study (remember, in many studies, the higher one is, the lower the other is). Also identify two or three issues that could threaten the internal validity of the study.

1. There is evidence suggesting that children's play with spatial toys (e.g., puzzles and blocks) correlates with spatial development. Females play less with spatial toys than do males, which arguably accounts for males' spatial advantages; children with high socioeconomic status (SES) also show an advantage, though SES-related differences in spatial play have been less studied than gender-related differences. Using a large, nationally representative sample from the standardization study of the Wechsler Preschool and Primary Scale of Intelligence–Fourth Edition, and controlling for other cognitive abilities, we observed a specific relation between parent-reported frequency of spatial play and Block Design scores that was invariant across gender and SES. Reported spatial play was higher for boys than for girls, but controlling for spatial play did not eliminate boys' relative advantage on this subtest. SES groups did not differ in reported frequency of spatial play. Future research should consider quality as well as quantity of play, and should explore underlying mechanisms to evaluate causality. (Jirout & Newcombe, 2015)

2. Although self-rated personality traits predict mortality risk, no study has examined whether one's friends can perceive personality characteristics that predict one's mortality risk. Moreover, it is unclear whether observers' reports (compared with self-reports) provide better or unique information concerning the personal characteristics that result in longer and healthier lives. To test whether friends' reports of personality predict mortality risk, we used data from a 75-year longitudinal study (the Kelly/Connolly Longitudinal Study on Personality and Aging). In that study, 600 participants were observed beginning in 1935 through 1938, when they were in their mid-20s, and continuing through 2013. Male participants seen by their friends as more conscientious and open lived longer, whereas friend-rated emotional stability and agreeableness were protective for women. Friends' ratings were better predictors of longevity than were self-reports of personality, in part because friends' ratings could be aggregated to provide a more reliable assessment. Our findings demonstrate the utility of observers' reports in the study of health and provide insights concerning the pathways by which personality traits influence health. (Jackson, Connolly, Garrison, Leveille, & Connolly, 2015)

3. We showed that anticipatory cognitive control could be unconsciously instantiated through subliminal cues that predicted enhanced future control needs. In task-switching experiments, one of three subliminal cues preceded each trial. Participants had no conscious experience or knowledge of these cues, but their performance was significantly improved on switch trials after cues that predicted task switches (but not particular tasks). This utilization of subliminal information was flexible and adapted to a change in cues predicting task switches and occurred only when switch trials were difficult and effortful. When cues were consciously visible, participants were unable to discern their relevance and could not use them to enhance switch performance. Our results show that unconscious cognition can implicitly use subliminal information in a goal-directed manner for anticipatory control, and they also suggest that subliminal representations may be more conducive to certain forms of associative learning. (Farooqui & Manly, 2015)

22. Learning Check—Experimental Designs

1. A psychologist is interested in the effect of peer pressure on risk-taking behaviors of college students. The psychologist designs an experiment to determine this effect where 200 students (who volunteer to serve as participants) are randomly placed in one of two situations. In each situation, five participants sit in a room with four other people. The four other people are actually confederates of the experimenter (i.e., they are part of the experiment), and their behavior is determined before the experiment begins. Half of the participants witness the four other people in the room leaning back in their chairs (a behavior that involves the minor risk of falling over backward in the chair). The other half of the participants also witness the four confederates leaning back in their chairs but are further encouraged by the confederates to exhibit the same behavior (e.g., they tell the subjects that leaning back is more comfortable, fun). The behavior of each participant is observed to determine whether they do or do not lean back in their chair during the experiment. For each group, the number of participants (out of five) who lean back in their chairs is recorded.

    a. List any independent variables in this study and the levels of each one.

    b. What is the dependent variable, and how is it being measured?

    c. What type of experimental design is this (e.g., bivalent, multivalent, or factorial)?

2. Explain why an experiment typically has higher internal validity but lower external validity than other research methods.

3. A research methods instructor wants to know if having students conduct their own research study as part of the course increases their understanding of major concepts in the course. To investigate this, she gives two sections of her course a pretest on the course concepts. She then gives one section a research study assignment for the course but does not give this assignment to her other section. At the end of the semester, she gives a posttest to both sections on the course concepts and compares the difference in the pretest-posttest scores as a measure of learning for the two sections of her course. The section with the research study assignment shows more learning. Explain why the instructor cannot be sure that the research study assignment *caused* more learning in this study.

23. Ethics Exercise

Pretend that you and your lab group are members of the **Institutional Review Board** (IRB). Read each research proposal below and evaluate the study for adherence to ethical principles of research conduct. Think about and answer the questions below to help you evaluate each study. Make suggestions, where possible, on how to improve the study to meet ethical guidelines.

    a. Does the study have scientific merit? How will society or the subjects of the study benefit?

    b. Does the study place subjects at risk for either physical or psychological harm? If it does, what aspects of the study cause this risk? Can you suggest less risky procedures that would still provide the researcher with the same information?

    c. Will subjects read and sign a consent form? If not, is there enough information given to the subjects to provide informed consent?

    d. Does the study use deception? If it does, will the subjects be fully debriefed? Can you think of a way for the researchers to answer the research question without using deception?

    e. Can the participants reasonably refuse to participate or withdraw during the study? If not, what part of the study appears to be coercive?

    f. Will the subjects' data be kept confidential?

    g. Do you have any other concerns about the study? If so, what are they?

Study 1. The current study will examine the idea that exercise will interfere with performance in an attention task. In the experiment, participants will be strapped to a treadmill while they also respond verbally to images on a computer screen. The experimenter will control the speed of the treadmill during the experiment. The participant will also be told that the experiment takes 1 hour and that they will receive $250 if they successfully complete the experiment. All participants will sign a consent form if they wish to participate. To avoid distractions during the experiment, the participants will run in a soundproof room and no communication between the participants and the experimenter will be allowed after the experiment has started. However, as a safety precaution, the experimenter will continuously monitor the participants' heart rates. After the participant is given instructions, the participant will be strapped to a restraining device that is connected to the treadmill. The participants' task will be to respond to target stimuli by verbally identifying the objects presented. The participants will be fully debriefed after the experiment.

Study 2. This study will examine conflict resolution behaviors between romantic couples. Participants will be romantic couples who have been dating at least 6 months. They will be asked to separately fill out questions about personal topics (e.g., sexual behaviors, drug and alcohol behaviors). Then the couple will be placed in a room together and asked to talk about an issue in their relationship. The session will be videotaped and later coded for conflict resolution behaviors by the experimenter. To be able to match the questionnaires with the tapes of the sessions, participants will be asked to put their name on the questionnaires when they complete them.

Study 3. In order to test the effects of control of eating behaviors on stress responses, rats will be run in pairs through an experiment. One rat in the pair will be presented with food whenever it makes the correct response in a discrimination task. A second rat will be presented with food at random times (i.e., not connected to its behavior). The rats and their food will be visible to each other during the experiment. Immediately after the experimental session, the rats will be removed from the test chambers and sacrificed. Their stomachs will be inspected for ulcers. The study will determine if the rats that lack control over the availability of food develop more stomach ulcers than the other rats. This information may have implications for health of humans with different eating habits. Therefore, the important information this study will provide justifies the use of shock treatments to the animals.

Study 4. In a simulation training study, undergraduate participants will be asked to help another participant learn a list of words. In reality, though, the participant learning the words will be an experimenter confederate who purposely gets some of the words wrong. The actual participants will be told that they have to scold the learner whenever the learner makes a mistake. Anytime the participants hesitate in scolding the learner for mistakes, the experimenter will tell them that they must scold the learner or they will not receive credit for the experiment. The number of times the participants scold the learners will be recorded. Each participant will sign a consent form before the experiment begins.

24. Ethics Exercise Paper

Download and read the following article:

Cantlon, J. F., & Brannon, E. M. (2006). Shared system for ordering small and large numbers in monkeys and humans. *Psychological Science, 17,* 401–406.

Questions to answer about the article:

1. Summarize the research question, the basic procedure used, and the results of the research.

2. What ethical issues did the researchers need to address for the human participants in this study?

3. What ethical issues did the researchers need to address for the nonhuman subjects in this study?

4. Even though all of the participants were in the same study (Experiment 2), the researchers face different ethical issues with the two groups. Compare and contrast the ethical issues of the two groups of participants.

25. Sample Consent Form

Participant's Informed Consent

Large Midwestern University

Dept. of Psychology

Principal Investigator: Dr. J. Q. Scientist

The policy of the Department of Psychology is that all research participation in the department is voluntary, and you have the right to withdraw at any time, without prejudice, should you object to the nature of the research. Your responses are confidential. Any report of the data collected will be in summary form, without identifying individuals. You are entitled to ask questions and to receive an explanation after your participation. You are free to withdraw your participation at any time without penalty. You must be 18 years of age to give your consent to participate in research.

Nature of Participation: You will participate in *1* session. In the session:

You will be presented with pairs of words. Your task will be to rate these word pairs with respect to how similar in meaning they are. The entire session will take less than an hour, and you will receive 1 hour of experimental credit for your participation.

Purpose of the Study: We are interested in how people understand and produce language. We are only interested in an evaluation of these variables and how they are related to one another. We are NOT interested in any specific individual.

Possible Risks: There are few psychological or physical risks involved in the present study. However, you may stop your participation in the study at any time without penalty. In rare occasions, you may feel frustrated if you make errors during the experiment. This is normal; please just perform as best as you can. You are entitled to take a copy of the informed consent form; however, we will also keep a copy in our files. There is a small chance of the loss of confidentiality; however, several procedures have been used to minimize this risk. You will be assigned a code number to protect your identity. All data will be kept in secured files, locked in the laboratory, in accord with the standards of the university, federal regulations, and the American Psychological Association. All identifying information will be removed from data files as soon as the data collection is complete.

Possible Benefits: (A) When your participation is complete, you will be given an opportunity to learn about this research, which may be useful to you in your course or in understanding yourself and others. (B) You will have an opportunity to contribute to psychological science by participating in this research. (C) You have the opportunity to earn credit in your course. See your instructor for details.

Confidentiality: You will be randomly assigned an ID number, which will protect your identity. All data will be kept in secured files, in accord with the standards of the university, federal regulations, and the American Psychological Association. No identifying information will be stored with your data. Finally, remember that it is no individual person's responses that interest us; we are studying language skills for people in general.

Opportunities to Question: Any technical questions about this research may be directed to the **Principal Investigator:** <u>Dr. J. Q. Scientist</u> **Phone:** <u>XXX-XXXX.</u> Data should be fully available by January 1, 20XX. Any questions regarding your rights as a research participant or research-related injuries may be directed to the University Office of Research, Ethics, and Compliance, <u>XXX-XXXX</u>.

Opportunities to Withdraw at Will: If you decide now or at any point to withdraw this consent or stop participating, you are free to do so at no penalty to yourself. You are free to skip specific questions and continue participating with no penalty.

I have read the statements above, understand the same, and voluntarily sign this form. I further acknowledge that I have received an offer of a copy of this consent form.

_____   _____

Signature of Participant   **Date**

26. Learning Check—Ethics

1. Explain what is involved in obtaining informed consent from a research participant.

2. How does the informed consent process differ for participants who are young children?

3. Explain what it means for a researcher to conduct a "risk-benefit analysis."

4. Explain what the purpose of an institutional review board (IRB) is.

5. Describe some differences in ethical guidelines for human and nonhuman subjects.

6. An instructor is interested in studying the use of cell phones in his classroom. He wants to have a teaching assistant record the number of times he sees students using their cell phones during class time. Describe some ethical issues that the instructor will need to consider before conducting this study.

27. Subject Sampling Exercise

Interpreting Poll Results: A Sampling Methodology Exercise

1. Find a report about a poll from a newspaper or the Internet (e.g., http://people-press.org/) and summarize the main findings.

2. Discuss how the respondents were sampled.

3. Discuss the strengths and potential weaknesses of the sampling method used in the study.

4. How is your interpretation of the results affected by the sampling method used?

28. Descriptive Statistics Exercise

Instructions: Below are data from a fictional two-factor experiment. Compute mean and standard deviation for each condition according to the instructions given. In addition, compute the marginal means for both factors.

Dr. Readalot conducted a study examining the effectiveness of different kinds of studying. He had students study either for 5 hours the night before the test (crammed study) or for 1 hour each of the five nights prior to the test (distributed study). Additionally, he was interested in whether the kind of material being studied (and tested) would interact with the method of studying (math or vocabulary). He tested five participants in each of the four conditions. The test score (in percentage correct) for each participant is presented in the table below. Follow the instructions given below the table.

Factor A: Math v. Vocabulary questions Factor B: Crammed v. Distributed practice				Marginal means for type of studying
		Math	Vocabulary	
Crammed		87	90	
		65	84	
		72	72	
		73	78	
		53	76	
	M: SD:	_____	M: SD: _____	
Distributed		88	98	
		75	89	
		82	79	
		75	84	
		80	100	
	M: SD:	_____	M: SD: _____	
Marginal means for type of material				

Marginal means for type of material

1. Compute the Crammed Math condition mean. Record your answer into the table on the previous page.

   Step 1: Add up the five scores.

   Step 2: Divide the total by 5 (the number of scores).

2. Do the same for the other three conditions. Record your answers into the table.

Step 1: Subtract the mean from each score in the condition (these are the **deviations**).	Step 2: Square each of the deviations.	Step 3: Add up the squared deviations (**sum of squared deviations**, SS).	Step 4: Divide SS by n – 1 (number of scores – one). This gives you **variance**.	Step 5: Take the square root of variance. This gives you your **standard deviation**.
87 – ___ = ___	___			
65 – ___ = ___	___	___	___ = ___	√___ = ___
72 – ___ = ___	___		(5–1)	
73 – ___ = ___	___			
53 – ___ = ___	___			

3. Compute the Crammed Math condition standard deviation. Record your answer into the table.

4. Do the same for the other three conditions. Record your answers into the table.

5. Compute the marginal means for study method. Record your answers into the table.

   Add up all of the scores in the crammed condition (that's 10 scores, 5 from math and 5 from vocabulary). Then divide by 10 (the total number of scores in the crammed condition). Repeat the process for distributed studying.
   (Hint: Don't just add the two means together and divide by 2. This will work for this example, but only because there are equal numbers of scores in the two conditions. If there are unequal numbers in your conditions, you will get the wrong number.)

6. Repeat the process to compute the marginal means for the material type. Record your answers into the table.

29. Graphing Exercise

A study has been conducted to compare men and women on the likelihood of seeking counseling for a psychological problem. A survey was completed by 1,000 men and 1,000 women to determine the number of each group suffering from anxiety or depression. The survey also asked if the respondent had sought counseling for his or her anxiety or depression. The mean values below indicate the percentage of those reporting one of the psychological problems who also sought counseling.

	Anxiety	Depression
Men	35%	15%
Women	20%	55%

1. Complete the bar graph below by including a point in the graph for each mean value given above. Be sure to connect lines for each gender.

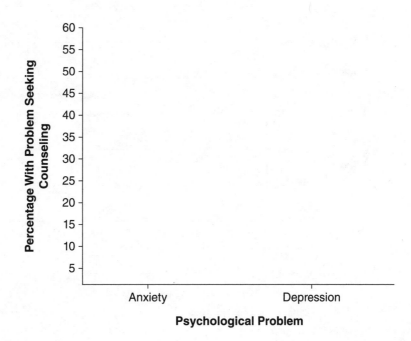

2. Re-create the graph above as a bar graph using a software package such as Excel. If using Excel, type in the means and variable levels as given above into a new worksheet, highlight what you have typed, and choose Insert Chart. Under Chart Type, you can choose a bar graph. Chart Options allow you to label the axes and adjust axis scales and fonts.

3. Describe in your own words the results displayed in the graphs.

30. Correlations and Scatterplots Exercise

1. Josie conducted an honors research project in which she measured IQ scores and number of hours spent watching TV per week for several students. Her results are shown below. Each pair of numbers represents one student. The IQ score is shown first, and the number of hours of TV watched per week is shown next (for both variables, a higher score means more).

   a. On the graph shown, plot the data points for each student. Label each axis of the graph to indicate the variable plotted.

   b. Below the graph, identify the relationship as either positive, negative, or no correlation.

   c. Estimate the numerical correlation value (r) as a number between –1.0 and +1.0. Write your r estimate below the graph.

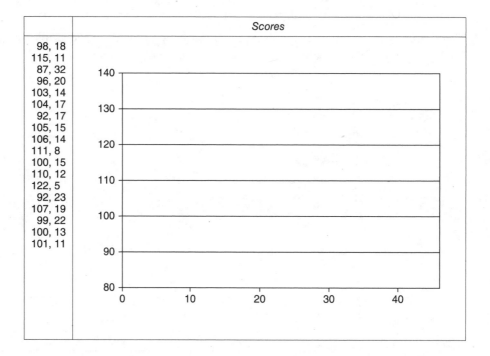

Scores
98, 18
115, 11
87, 32
96, 20
103, 14
104, 17
92, 17
105, 15
106, 14
111, 8
100, 15
110, 12
122, 5
92, 23
107, 19
99, 22
100, 13
101, 11

2. Each pair of variables below has a known relationship. Use common sense to determine what type of relationship likely exists between the variables.

   a. The number of times per day you smile at other people and the number of times per day others smile at you.

   b. The number of hours per day a person studies and the number of exams per semester a person fails.

   c. The number of gallons of water a person drinks in a week and the number of close friends the person has.

   d. The number of alcoholic drinks a person has each week and the person's GPA.

31. Inferential Statistics Exercise

Part 1: Making Hypotheses

For each study described below, state the null hypothesis. Then review the results for the study and decide what your decision (accept or reject) should be with regard to the two hypotheses. Remember, you should NEVER accept a null hypothesis.

Study 1

Alternative Hypothesis: Anxiety increases lying in children.

a. *Null hypothesis:*

Study 1 results: A study compared 50 children who were placed in an anxiety-inducing situation with 50 children in a control group. They were then asked about their behavior, and the number of inaccurate responses was recorded. Inaccurate responses did not differ for the two groups.

b. We should _____ the null hypothesis.

c. We should _____ the scientific hypothesis.

d. Suppose that the study described above was conducted inaccurately and that anxious children really do lie more. In this case, we have made a

Type I   **Type II** (circle one) decision error.

Study 2

Alternative Hypothesis: People are more likely to help a stranger if there is no one else around than if they are in a group (i.e., the bystander effect).

a. *Null hypothesis:*

Study 2 results: A situation was set up on a busy highway where someone needed help with her car. Researchers observed 100 cars drive by and counted the number of people who stopped and whether they were alone or with other people in the car. People driving with others stopped less often to help than people who were driving alone.

b. We should _____ the null hypothesis.

c. We should _____ the scientific hypothesis.

d. Suppose that the above study contains a confounding variable, and when tested properly, people driving with others actually stop just as often as people driving alone. In this case, the study described above has led us to make a

Type I   **Type II** (circle one) decision error.

Whenever we reject the null hypothesis, what does this tell us about the independent variable?

Part 2: Inferential Statistics

Study 3

A behavioral psychologist conducts an experiment to determine whether operant conditioning techniques can be used to improve balance in people who consider themselves "clumsy." She recruits 50 participants, each of whom responds yes to the question "Do you consider yourself clumsy?" on a pre-experimental questionnaire. Half the participants are given a balance task (stand on one foot with your arms in the air) with the time they can balance recorded. They are then excused and asked to return 3 weeks later. The other half of the participants are given 3 weeks of operant training during a balance exercise. In this training, the participants are asked to perform the balance task described above. Each time they can beat their previous balance time, they receive $10. After the 3-week period, all participants are asked to perform the balance task again. Alpha is set at .05. The members of the Training Group can balance for an average of 25 seconds. Members of the Control Group (who did not receive the training) can balance for an average of 24.3 seconds. When the inferential statistical test is conducted on these data, $p = .08$.

1. What is the IV for this study? The DV?

2. What is the alternative hypothesis?

3. What is the null hypothesis?

4. What *population* is being tested in this study?

5. Is the difference observed in the study statistically significant? Why or why not?

6. Based on your answer to (5) above, what decision should be made about the null hypothesis?

7. In the context of this experiment, what *exactly* is p the probability of?

Study 4

Some have claimed that children of divorced parents are not as well adjusted as children of parents who are married. To test this idea, you set up a study with two groups. One group consists of 100 children who have divorced parents. The other group consists of 100 children who have married parents. Each child in the study is asked to complete the Social Adjustment Scale for Children (SASC). Higher scores on the scale indicate better social adjustment.

1. Does this study contain an independent variable? Why or why not?

2. What dependent variable is measured in this study?

3. What is the null hypothesis for this study?

4. What is the alternative hypothesis?

The results indicate a mean difference of 10 on the SASC scale between the two groups of children. With alpha set at .05, $p = .02$.

5. What decision should be made with regard to the null hypothesis?

6. Describe one possible source of bias that could be present in this study causing the results that were observed.

32. Inferential Statistics and Analysis Exercise

Listed below are 10 statements that are common pieces of cliché advice (many of which you may have heard at some point in your life). Pick two of the clichés, and design a study to test each one following the example provided below.

Absence makes the heart grow fonder.	Experience is the best teacher.
All work and no play make Jack a very dull boy.	An apple never falls far from the tree.
Good fences make good neighbors.	He who laughs last, laughs longest.
Ignorance is bliss.	A rose by any other name still smells as sweet.
Opposites attract (relationships).	An apple a day keeps the doctor away.

Example: Laughter is the best medicine.

> **Tails** (circle one): (One-Tailed)   Two-Tailed

> **Null Hypothesis:** Within the population, laughter is not the best medicine (is worse or as good as without it).

> **Alternative Hypothesis:** Within the population, laughter is the best medicine.

> **Independent Variables:** Laughter (presence vs. absence), Time health is measured (start and end of study)

> **Dependent Variable:** Physiological and Psychological Health

> **Details:** Between-Subjects, (Within-Subjects,) or Mixed?

>> **Why?** Laughter should be done between-subjects to avoid order effects. Time is a within-subjects variable because all subjects will receive the measures twice.

Analysis Plan

One Sample *t*-test   **Why?** This is a factorial design with 2 IVs so you need a two-way ANOVA.

Paired samples *t*-test

Independent Samples *t*-test

One-Way ANOVA

(Two-Way ANOVA)

Cliché #1: _____

_____

_____

Tails (circle one): One-Tailed   Two-Tailed

Null Hypothesis: _____

Alternative Hypothesis: _____

Independent Variable(s): _____

Dependent Variable(s): _____

Details: Between-Subjects, Within-Subjects, or Mixed?

　　Why? _____

_____

_____

_____

_____

Analysis Plan

One Sample *t*-test　　　　　Why? _____

Paired Samples *t*-test　　　　_____

Independent Samples *t*-test　_____

One-Way ANOVA　　　　　　_____

Two-Way ANOVA　　　　　　_____

Cliché #2:_____

_____

_____

    Tails (circle one): One-Tailed   Two-Tailed

    Null Hypothesis: _____

    Alternative Hypothesis: _____

    Independent Variable(s): _____

    Dependent Variable(s): _____

    Details: Between-Subjects, Within-Subjects, or Mixed?

        Why?_____

_____

_____

_____

_____

    Analysis Plan

One Sample *t*-test   Why? _____

Paired Samples *t*-test   _____

Independent Samples *t*-test   _____

One-Way ANOVA   _____

Two-Way ANOVA   _____

33. Hypothesis Generation Exercise

For each of the following research descriptions:

    a. write out the null and scientific (alternative) hypotheses

    b. indicate whether a one-tailed or two-tailed statistical test should be performed

    c. identify the dependent variable and the scale used to measure it

1. IQ scores for the general population form a normal distribution with a mean of 100 and a standard deviation of 15. However, there are data that indicate that children's intelligence can be affected if their mothers had German measles during pregnancy. Using hospital records, a researcher obtained a sample of schoolchildren whose mothers all had German measles during their pregnancies. The researcher wants to test whether the children in the sample have an average IQ lower than that of the general population.

2. Suppose we think that listening to classical music will affect the amount of time it takes a person to fall asleep. An experimenter randomly assigns participants to one of two groups. Both groups of participants are asked to spend two nights sleeping in the researcher's laboratory. On the second night, one group goes to sleep listening to classical music, while the other goes to sleep in silence (the first night is used to allow the participants a chance to become accustomed to sleeping while wearing the sleep-monitoring equipment). The researcher measures the time span between when the lights are turned off and the onset of stage 2 sleep.

3. A developmental psychologist believes that a new technique can help kids learn math skills faster than the current technique. He measures math skills of two groups of fifth graders using a standardized math skills test (higher scores on the test correspond to stronger math skills). For one group of kids, the psychologist uses the new technique. For the other group, he uses the standard math curriculum.

4. A psychologist examines the effect of chronic alcohol abuse on memory. The researcher obtains a sample of alcohol abusers and finds that the group averaged a mean score of 47 on a standardized memory test. In comparison, scores on the memory test are normally distributed around a mean of 50 (standard deviation of 6) for the general population. Is there evidence for memory impairment among alcoholics?

5. On a vocational interest inventory that measures interest in several categories, a very large standardization group of adults (i.e., a population) has an average score of 22 (higher scores represent greater interest). A researcher would like to determine if scientists differ from the general population in terms of writing interests. The researcher administers the test to a random sample of scientists (selected from the directory of a national science society). The test scores on the literary scale for the scientists are compared to those of the general population to examine the question of whether scientists differ from the general population in their writing interests.

34. Statistics With Excel Exercise

Statistics are a central tool of researchers. Fortunately, there are many computer statistical programs available designed to help us "crunch the numbers." One widely available program is Microsoft's Excel. Excel is a spreadsheet program that can be used by researchers to manage and analyze data sets. The following exercise is designed to introduce you to some of the basic descriptive and inferential statistical resources within Excel that may be useful in Research Methods courses.

Suppose that we conducted an experiment comparing a treatment group with a control group. We could enter the data into Excel as an array of numbers.

	A	B	C
	A	*B*	*C*
1	Control	Treatment	
2	45	64	
3	65	76	
4	75	83	
5	56	69	
6	46	66	
7			
8			
9			
10			

Now that the data are entered, you can perform a number of operations.

Suppose that you wanted to compute the mean of the control group. You can do this in several different ways. One way would be to enter the equation. For example, in the A7 cell, you can enter:

$$= (A2 + A3 + A4 + A5 + A6)/5$$

This will return the mean of these five numbers.

You can do most any of your statistical analyses of your data by entering the appropriate equations (sometimes using multiple steps, e.g., compute the mean first, then use it to compute the standard deviation, then use that to compute your standard error). However, Excel also has several statistical functions built into it. Some of the most common ones include (and can be found under the insert menu: Function):

Descriptive statistics:

= Sum (array)

= Average (array) *Mean*

= Median (array) *Median*

= StDevA (array) *StandardDeviation (sample)*

= StDevP (array) *StandardDeviation (population)*

(*Notice:* Array in this case would be something like A2:A6 to mean A2, A3, A4, A5, and A6.)

Excel also includes some inferential statistical procedures.

t-test: = ttest(array1,array2,tails,type)

For the first equation, you must arrange the data into two arrays for this analysis.

(tails = 1 or 2 for 1-tailed or 2-tailed)

(type = 1, 2, or 3 for paired test, independent samples with equal variances, independent samples with unequal variance)

(*Notice:* The value that is returned is the *p* value, not the computed *t*-score)

correlation: = correl(array1,array2)

You must arrange the data into two arrays of the same size for this analysis.

Exercise Using Excel

Enter the data set from the above example into an Excel spreadsheet.

1. Using Excel, compute the mean and sample standard deviation for each group.

2. Using Excel, compute the correlation between two groups.

3. Using Excel, compute a paired samples *t*-test. Based on your results, using an alpha level of 0.05 and a 2-tailed test, should you reject the null hypothesis?

35. Learning Check—Statistics

1. Define the concept of sampling error and explain why it is important for hypothesis testing.

2. What two types of errors can be made during hypothesis testing? Describe how each error is made.

3. What two descriptive statistics are most important in calculating an inferential statistic?

4. Determine the mean and mode for the data set listed below:

$$\underline{X}$$
5
6
3
5
6
4
3
$$\underline{3}$$

Mean

Mode

5. Suppose a study had been conducted to compare adolescent boys and girls on their dating experiences. Fifty 15-year-olds reported the number of times they had romantic involvement with someone else in the past 6 months, where romantic involvement was operationally defined as dating, sexual contact of any sort, or conversing with someone they were romantically interested in. Boys reported a mean number of 25 incidents, and girls reported a mean number of 14.5 incidents. A statistical test was conducted to compare incident scores for the two groups.

a. What is the null hypothesis for this study? What is the alternative hypothesis?

b. What is the appropriate statistical test for comparing boys and girls on this measure?

c. The statistical test gave a p value of .013. Assuming alpha = .05, what decision should be made with regard to the null hypothesis?

6. A researcher wants to know if connecting a smell to studied information aids memory. Subjects are asked to study a list of words. For one group, a distinctive smell (different flowers, soap, etc.) is presented with each word. For the other group, no smells are presented with the words. The researcher finds that the group that receives the smells recalls 75% of the words, and the group without smells recalls 69% of the words.

a. What is the null hypothesis for this study? What is the alternative hypothesis?

b. What is the appropriate statistical test for comparing memory for the two groups?

c. Suppose that all subjects had received smells with half of the words presented and no smells for the other half of the words they saw. In this new design, what would be the appropriate statistical test to use?

d. The statistical test gave a p value of .09. Assuming alpha = .05, what decision should be made with regard to the null hypothesis?

36. Bias and Control Exercise

For each study description below, list possible confounding variables that might be present in the study based on the description provided.

1. A researcher wanted to determine whether different forms of exercise improve memory and problem-solving skills, with the hope of helping treat elderly people with cognitive impairments. She recruited 10 members of the swim team and 10 members of the track team at a local college to be tested on two types of tasks. Each group received a memory task that involved memorizing a list of 10 words and recalling them, and a problem-solving task that involved solving anagrams of these same 10 words (an anagram is a jumbled word that needs to be rearranged, like HBCEA for BEACH). The swim team received the memory task followed by the problem-solving task, and the track team received the problem-solving task followed by the memory task. Each group was tested 15 minutes after its respective team practices (either swim or track). The results showed a significant interaction in that members of the swim team performed significantly better on the problem-solving task than the track team, and the members of the track team performed significantly better on the memory task than the swim team members. The researcher concluded that to help elderly people with their problem-solving skills, they should swim more, and to help with their memory, elderly people should take up running or jogging.

2. Tsapelas, Aron, and Orbuch (2009) recently conducted a study to examine the effects of boredom on marital satisfaction. Participants included 123 couples. Couples were questioned separately in their homes after 7 years of marriage and after 16 years of marriage. At each session, couples were asked to rate how much they felt their marriage was "in a rut" and how satisfied they were with their marriage. Results of the study indicated that boredom with marriage at 7 years was related to a decrease in martial satisfaction at 16 years.

3. A social psychologist is interested in studying the effect of the size of a group on problem solving. She conducts the experiment in her two Introductory Psychology courses. During a class exercise in each class, she asks students to form groups of two, five, or eight to work on the activity. She records how quickly each group finishes the task. She conducts related samples *t*-tests to compare the completion times for the three group sizes. She finds that groups of size two finished faster than the other two groups and groups of size five finished faster than groups of size eight.

For each description below, read the description of the study and then answer the questions about the sources of bias and how to control for them.

4. I want to conduct an experiment to determine the effect of instructional mode on learning. I have students learn material either in a computer-based interactive environment or by reading a traditional text. One group of students gets the computer-based instruction, and the other group reads the text. Both groups are presented with the same material and spend the same amount of time learning the material. Both groups are given the same test at the completion of learning. I find that the group with the computer-based instruction scores higher on the final test. However, I have a confound of previous knowledge of the students in my experiment, so my results are not valid. Think of a few different ways I can redesign my experiment to control for this confounding.

5. I have designed an experiment to learn how attention processes operate in search tasks. I present participants with a display that contains letters placed in random positions on a computer screen. The participants' task is to find a colored X among a field of other letters. Participants are to report the color of the X when they find it on the screen. I am interested in how the shapes of the distractors (the other letters) affect the speed of the task. To determine this, I first run participants through a set of 50 trials where all of the distractors are rounded letters (such as O and Q) and then I run them through a set of 50 trials where all of the distractors contain straight lines (such as T and K). For the rounded distractors, I use Xs that are blue, red, or yellow. For straight-line distractors, I use Xs that are green, brown, or orange. I have a set of similar participants (education, visual abilities, etc.), and I have controlled for the number of each type of letter serving as a distractor. The presentation timing of all trials is exactly the same. I find that participants are slower on the trials with straight-line letters as distractors. I have two major confounds in this experiment, which makes my data invalid. One is the order in which the participants are given the two letter conditions. What is the other? How can I redesign my experiment to control for these sources of bias?

37. Factorial Design Exercise

1. Consider the following data from a factorial-design experiment. The DV was "% of participants who offered help to a stranger in distress."

	Gender of Stranger	
Number of Bystanders	Male	Female
0	30	90
10	10	50

a. What is the design of this study (e.g., 2 × 2, 2 × 3, etc.)?

b. List the independent variables of this study, and list the levels of each.

c. Sketch a graph of the results of the study. Fill in the names and levels of the IVs.

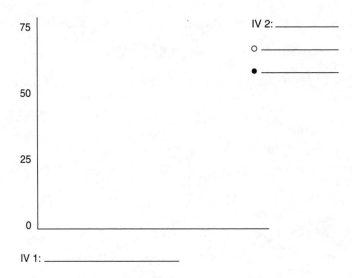

d. Main effects
  - On the average, how does the number of bystanders affect helping?

  - On the average, how does the gender of the stranger in need affect helping?

e. Do the graphed data suggest the presence of an interaction effect? If so, describe it.

2. In the factorial design experiment summarized below, the dependent variable was "Average number of hallucinations."

	Type of Drug	
Dose of drug	LSD	Marijuana
Low	3	1
Medium	5	2
High	13	3

a. What is the design of this study (e.g., 2 × 2, 2 × 3, etc.)?

b. Sketch a graph of the results of the study. Fill in the names.

c. *Main effects:* For each factor and levels of the IVs, state whether a main effect appears to exist. If one does, describe it.

d. Do the graphed data suggest the presence of an interaction effect? If so, describe it.

38. Factorial Design Exercise— Sproesser, Schupp, and Renner (2014)

Reference:

Sproesser, G., Schupp, H. T., & Renner, B. (2014). The bright side of stress-induced eating: Eating more when stressed but less when pleased. *Psychological Science, 25,* 58–65.

The researchers in this study were interested in how social situations can influence stress-induced eating. They grouped subjects according to self-reported stress-induced eating habits: consistently eating more (hyperphagics) or eating less (hypophagics) when stressed. Each subject was then exposed to one of three social situations: (1) a social inclusion condition, where subjects were told that a confederate partner had approved of a video they had made answering some questions and was looking forward to meeting them, (2) a neutral condition, where they were told their partners could not meet them because their partners had to cancel their participation, or (3) a social exclusion condition, where they were told that their partner had decided not to meet them after viewing their video. Subjects were then given an ice cream taste test and the amount of ice cream consumed was measured.

Use this description to help you answer the questions below.

1. What is the independent variable in this study, and what are its levels?

2. The researchers also included a subject/attribute variable in this study. What was this subject variable? How were subjects classified on this variable?

The results of the experiment are displayed in the graph below:

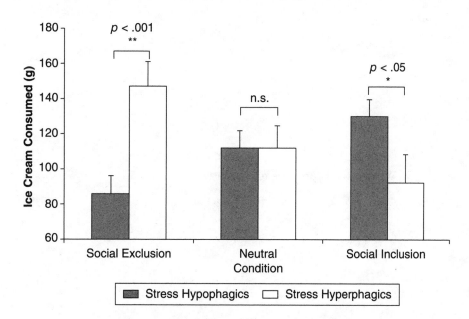

3. Does this graph indicate a main effect of social condition? Explain your answer.

4. Does this graph indicate a main effect of eating phagic group? Explain your answer.

5. Does this graph indicate the presence of an interaction? If so, describe the interaction.

39. Factorial Design Exercise— Farmer, McKay, and Tsakiris (2014)

For this exercise, download the article referenced below (it can be found on the SAGE Student Site):

Farmer, H., McKay, R., & Tsakiris, M. (2014). Trust in me: Trustworthy others are seen as more physically similar to the self. *Psychological Science, 25,* 290–292.

1. Describe the study. Make sure to include the following information:

   - What is/are the dependent variable(s)?
   - What is/are the independent variable(s)?
   - For each independent variable, how many levels does it have?
   - For each independent variable, is it manipulated between or within groups?
   - How many total conditions are there in the study?

2. What are the hypotheses for each independent variable (main effect predictions)?

3. What is the hypothesis for the interaction?

The results presented in the graph below show the mean percentage of the trustee's face that was present in the photos judged to be at (PSE) as a function of the conditions of the experiment.

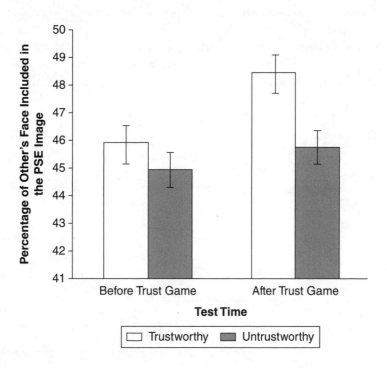

4. Describe the pattern of results seen in the graph. Does the pattern suggest that an interaction is present? If so, describe the interaction; if not, describe why the pattern does not indicate an interaction.

5. What do the statistical outcomes in the Results section tell you about the main effects and interaction? (*Note:* this question should only be answered if downloading the article and reading the Results section was assigned).

6. What do these results tell us about the hypotheses for this study?

40. Describing Main Effects and Interactions Exercise

The following data sets are from a factorial design study examining the effects of group and individual therapy over two different lengths of time. For each data set, determine what effects (both main effects and the interaction) are significant. For simplicity, assume that the data are ideal, meaning that any difference between means is a significant difference—no sampling error. Make a bar graph of each significant effect and provide a verbal description of the effect.

a.

	Therapy Type	
Length	Group	Individual
1 week	100	100
6 weeks	500	500

b.

	Therapy Type	
Length	Group	Individual
1 week	300	700
6 weeks	200	400

c.

	Therapy Type	
Length	Group	Individual
1 week	100	400
6 weeks	400	100

d.

	Therapy Type	
Length	Group	Individual
1 week	250	100
6 weeks	250	400

41. Specialized Designs Exercise: Developmental

Below are the reference and an adapted abstract of a published research paper.

- Identify the kind of specialized developmental design that was used in the study.
- Identify the variables (e.g., dependent, independent, quasi-independent, and control) that were studied.
- What are the advantages of using this specialized design?
- How could you redesign the study using a different specialized developmental design? What would be the advantages and disadvantages of using this alternative design?

Plomin, R., Fulker, D. W., Corley, R., & DeFries, J. C. (1997). Nature, nurture, and cognitive development from 1 to 16 years: A parent-offspring adoption study. *Psychological Science, 8,* 442–447.

Adapted Abstract

Studied 245 adopted children and their biological and adoptive parents, as well as 245 matched non-adoptive parents and offspring to examine genetic versus environmental influences on cognitive development over a 20-year span. The children were tested at 1, 2, 3, 4, 7, 12, and 16 years of age using standard intelligence tests. Results show that the adopted children resembled their adoptive parents slightly in early childhood but not at all in middle childhood or adolescence. In contrast, during childhood and adolescence adopted children become more like their biological parents, and to the same degree as children and parents in control families. Although these results were strongest for general cognitive ability and verbal ability, similar results were found for other specific cognitive abilities such as spatial ability, speed of processing, and recognition memory. These findings indicate that, within this population, genes that affect cognitive abilities in adulthood do not all come into play until adolescence and that environmental factors that contribute to cognitive development are not correlated with parents' cognitive ability.

42. Learning Check—Bias and Control and Specialized Designs

1. I want to design a study to determine the effects of age on quantity of social interaction. I will measure how many friends each of my participants reports they speak to on a given day. I will use three groups of participants: 8- to 10-year-olds, 12- to 15-year-olds, and 17- to 18-year-olds. Thirty participants will be in each group. I am using a cohort-sequential design.

   a. Describe how I might change this study to use a longitudinal design.

   b. Can I determine if age causes a change in quantity of social interactions with this study? Why or why not?

   c. List one possible covariate that I might use in this study to remove some of the variability in the data.

2. I want to conduct a study to determine at what age (if any) an instructional technique given to 2nd, 5th, and 9th grade classes improves learning. The instructional technique will be used for 6 months in each class. Describe how I would design this study as a cross-sectional design. What type of design should I use if I want to measure learning? What will my dependent variable be in this design?

3. You want to conduct an experiment to determine the effect of running on verbal ability. You ask participants to run 1 mile and then state all the words they can in a 30-second period. List two confounding variables that you should consider controlling for in this experiment and how you might control for them in the design.

4. For each design type listed below, state one advantage and one disadvantage of using that design:

   a. within-subjects design

   b. longitudinal design

   c. small-*n* design

5. Describe how you would conduct an interrupted time series design to determine if the public's trust of politicians changed after September 11, 2001.

6. How do discrete trials and baseline small-n designs differ?

7. Suppose you are a school psychologist working in an elementary school. A teacher has come to ask for your help with a student who has been disruptive to her class by consistently getting out of her seat, talking without raising her hand, and refusing to work on activities with a group. You propose a reward system for the student such that she receives a sticker for each time she is exhibiting appropriate classroom behavior (e.g., staying in her seat for a segment of the class, talking after raising her hand, working cooperatively with a group in an activity). She can then redeem a set number of stickers for small prizes from her parents (e.g., small stuffed animals). Describe how you might implement this reward system for the student in an A-B-A design to determine if it is effective in increasing appropriate classroom behaviors for her.

PART II

Research Project Exercises

In the second component, a research development project is included that can be assigned to groups or individuals and completed throughout the course as students learn the steps in designing research studies. This component includes assignments related to choosing a research topic, conducting a literature review, developing a method, analyzing and interpreting results, and presentation of the project as an oral or poster presentation. These assignments progress through the topics in the course and thus can be assigned at different points in the course after different topics have been covered that allow students to continue in their development of the project.

43. Getting Your Research Ideas for the Group Project

Write down two or three possible ideas for your group research project.

1.

2.

3.

44. Picking Your Research Idea for the Group Project

Within your group, generate and discuss the research ideas you all generated. After ideas for the group projects have been presented and discussed, choose the project your group will conduct, and write a brief description of the project that your group picked by answering the questions below. Be prepared to present your idea to the class.

What is your research question? Try to state it in the form of a question you will attempt to answer with your study.

Briefly describe the general method of your study (as much as you know at this point).

45. Brief Literature Review for Group Project Development

Each member of the group must do a brief search of the literature and find at least two related research articles for the group project. List the full reference of the articles that you found below. Also bring a copy of each article to your group for discussion of the articles and their relevance to your project.

Reference 1:

Reference 2:

46. Variables in Your Group Projects

State your tentative hypothesis for your group project.

Will your study include independent variables?

If so, what is/are your independent variable(s) (at a conceptual level)? How do you plan to manipulate your independent variable(s)? How is/are your independent variable(s) operationally defined?

What is/are your dependent measure(s)? How will you measure it/them?

What confounding variables will you need to control? Why?

47. Mock Institutional Review Board Form

Complete the following IRB protocol form for the project you designed in your group.

I. General Information

A. *Protocol Information*
Protocol Title:

B. *Principal Investigator Information (list the members of your research group)*
Principal Investigators:

II. Principal Investigator Assurance

As **Principal Investigator, I certify that to the best of my knowledge:**

1. The information provided for this project is correct.

2. No other procedures will be used in this protocol.

3. I agree to conduct this research as described in the attached supporting documents.

4. I will request and receive approval from the IRB for changes prior to implementing these changes (including but not limited to changes in cooperating investigators, as well as any changes in procedures).

5. I will comply with the IRB and university policy for the conduct of ethical research.

6. I will be responsible for ensuring that the work of my co-investigator(s)/student researcher(s) complies with this protocol.

7. Any unexpected or otherwise significant adverse events in the course of this study will be promptly reported to the Research Office.

8. In the case of student research, I assume responsibility for ensuring that the student complies with university and federal regulations regarding the use of human subjects in research.

_____   _____

_____   _____

_____   _____

Principal Investigator   Signatures   Date

III. Protocol Description

A. Provide a *brief* description, in *layman's terms*, of the proposed research.

B. Methodology

   1. Participants

      a. How many participants will be included in the study?

         Number: Male _____ Female _____ Total _____

         Age range: _____ to _____

      b. Where will participants be recruited from?

      c. How will they be recruited?

      d. Procedure for securing informed consent:

2. Procedure

   a. What are you asking the participants to do?

   b. Will you involve them in a psychological intervention, deception, or biomedical procedure?

   c. Will you audio- or videotape them (if yes, indicate which one)?

3. Instruments/Apparatus

What forms, surveys, equipment, and so on will you use? (Attach a copy of all forms, surveys, and instruments to be used.)

4. Data
   a. How will the data be stored and kept secure?

   b. Who will have access? How will the data be used (during and after the research)?

   c. How will the data be disposed of?

C. Risks

1. What are the physical, psychological, or social (loss of reputation, privacy, or employability) risks?

2. Will the data be anonymous or confidential?

D. Benefits

1. What do you hope to learn?

2. Who might find these results useful?

3. For what purpose?

48. Pilot of Research Project

An important part of the research process is to "try out" your study in advance of data collection. Piloting the methods allows researchers to try out things (e.g., your materials, your procedures, your instructions, your sampling procedures) and to get feedback from participants (researchers can also act as participants to gain insightful feedback). For your group projects, you should conduct a "practice run" of your entire method (using either group members or naive, nonclass volunteers).

Based on your pilot, answer the following questions:

- How long does the entire procedure take?

- Were there any demand characteristics? What comments did the participants have about the study? Did they have predictions about what the study was about?

- Did the materials work? Did the instructions work?

Other comments/observations:

Based on the pilot, what changes (if any) need to be made?

49. Statistical Analyses for Your Group Project

What is the design of your study? Will you compare group mean scores or examine a relationship between variables?

Describe how you will organize your project data so that you will be able to perform the appropriate descriptive and inferential statistics.

What descriptive statistics do you plan to use?

What inferential statistics do you plan to use? (Remember that the design of your study will largely determine what inferential statistical procedures you will use.)

50. Group Project Literature Review

The goal of writing a research report is to inform and persuade the reader about the research. A critical part of the writing is to provide the reader with a good summary of what the issue is and what is and isn't known about the issue (i.e., past research). Using the collected background articles that your group project members assembled in the brief literature review you conducted earlier, put together an introduction and literature review. This should include:

- a clear statement of the problem (issue), what it is, and why it is interesting/important
- a brief review of relevant past research (based on the articles that your group found)

Make sure that you link the problem/issue and the past research (i.e., how is the reviewed research relevant to your project?). Also make sure that the entire introduction and literature review fit together (i.e., it is not just a list of article summaries). Also spell check, grammar check, and so on. The entire document should be typed with double spacing and should adhere to APA style guidelines. Additionally, I'd like you to turn in a copy of your reference section (all of the articles that you cited in your introduction/literature review).

Literature Review Checklist

Key points	✓	Brief comment
Content		
Introduction		
Problem of interest	❑	
Link between problem and past research	❑	
Summarize the past research	❑	
Describe the basic purpose of the current experiment	❑	
Describe hypotheses (conceptual level IV and DV)	❑	
Subtotal	_____%	
Writing		
Overall clarity	❑	
APA style	❑	
Grammar	❑	
Spelling	❑	
Total Summary Grade	_____%	

51. Group Project Methods Section

The goal of writing a research report is to inform and persuade the reader about the research. A critical part of the writing is to provide the reader with a clear summary of what was done in the research. Your Method section should include all the subsections of the Method section (e.g., participants, design, procedure). Make sure that you clearly identify your variables (dependent, independent, and control) and how you intend to measure and/or manipulate them. Also spell-check, grammar check, and so on. The entire document should be typed with double spacing and should adhere to APA style guidelines.

Method Section Review Checklist

Key points	✓	Brief comment
Content		
Method		
APA subsections	☐	
Participants (if you haven't run any yet, give a numerical estimate)	☐	
Design	☐	
Materials	☐	
Apparatus (if appropriate)	☐	
Procedure	☐	
Variables		
Dependent	☐	
Independent	☐	
Control	☐	
Subtotal	_____%	
Writing		
Overall clarity	☐	
APA style	☐	
Grammar	☐	
Spelling	☐	
Total Summary Grade	_____%	

52. Group Project Results Section

The goal of writing a research report is to inform and persuade the reader about the research. A critical part of the writing is to provide the reader with a clear summary of what was found. Your Results section should include all the descriptive and inferential statistics, including graphs and relevant tables. The entire document should be typed with double spacing and should adhere to APA style guidelines.

Results Section Checklist

Key points	✓	Brief comment
Content		
Results		
Descriptive statistics	❑	
Inferential statistics	❑	
Tables and graphs	❑	
Subtotal _____%		
Writing		
Overall clarity	❑	
APA style	❑	
Grammar	❑	
Spelling	❑	
Total Summary Grade _____%		

53. Group Project Discussion Section

The goal of writing a research report is to inform and persuade the reader about the research. A critical part of the writing is to provide the reader with a clear summary of what was found, why it is important, and how it relates to the previous research in the area. Your Discussion section should include a restatement of your hypotheses, whether the hypotheses were supported or not, and which results are relevant to your hypotheses. In addition, you should compare your results to previous studies in the area and summarize the contribution of your study. The entire document should be typed with double spacing and should adhere to APA style guidelines.

Discussion Section Checklist

Key points	✓	Brief comment
Content		
Discussion		
Were the hypotheses supported or rejected?	❑	
What are the implications of the results?	❑	
Discussion of possible alternative explanations	❑	
Future directions	❑	
Conclusions (optional)	❑	
Subtotal _____%		
Writing		
Overall clarity	❑	
APA style	❑	
Grammar	❑	
Spelling	❑	
Total Summary Grade _____%		

54. Group Project Abstract

The goal of writing a research report is to inform and persuade the reader about the research. The abstract is a brief summary of the article, allowing the reader to know what was done without reading the entire article. It is often the "first contact" that readers have with an article (e.g., it is often included in searchable databases such as PsycINFO). As is the case with the rest of the article, clarity is a critical part of the writing. The summary should include brief statements of the issues, the methods used, the results, and the conclusions. The entire abstract should be no more than 120 words in length. The entire document should be typed with double spacing and should adhere to APA style guidelines.

Abstract Checklist

Key points	✓	Brief comment
Content		
Main point of the research		
Relevant participant information	❑	
Basic methodology used	❑	
Main results	❑	
Conclusions	❑	
Subtotal	_____%	
Writing		
Overall clarity	❑	
APA style (including appropriate length)	❑	
Grammar	❑	
Spelling	❑	
Total Summary Grade	_____%	

55. Poster Presentation Checklist

Key points	✓	Brief comment
Content		
Introduction		
Problem of interest	☐	
Very brief summary of the past research	☐	
Describe the basic purpose of the current experiment	☐	
Describe hypotheses (conceptual level IV and DV)	☐	
Method		
Brief, but clear	☐	
Design—IVs and DVs, operational definitions	☐	
Materials—description of the stimuli	☐	
Procedure—how the study was performed	☐	
Results		
Descriptive statistics	☐	
Results of the inferential statistics (what is significant, what isn't)	☐	
Discussion		
Were the hypotheses supported or rejected?	☐	
What are the implications of the results?	☐	
Are there a manageable number of "take home" points?	☐	
References		
If sources are cited, are full references provided?	☐	
Tables and Figures		
Useful information for reader	☐	
Neat, easy to get the appropriate information	☐	
Subtotal	_____%	
Format		
Overall clarity	☐	
Font size	☐	
Balance of text and figures	☐	
Total Summary Grade	_____%	

56. Oral Presentation Checklist

Key points	✓	Brief comment
Content		
Introduction		
Problem of interest	❑	
Very brief summary of the past research	❑	
Describe the basic purpose of the current experiment	❑	
Describe hypotheses (conceptual level IV and DV)	❑	
Method		
Brief, but clear	❑	
Design—IVs and DVs, operational definitions	❑	
Materials—description of the stimuli	❑	
Procedure—how the study was performed	❑	
Results		
Descriptive statistics	❑	
Results of the inferential statistics (what is significant, what isn't)	❑	
Discussion		
Were the hypotheses supported or rejected?	❑	
What are the implications of the results?	❑	
Are there a manageable number of "take home" points?	❑	
Citations		
Were proper citations provided where appropriate?	❑	
Tables and Figures		
Useful information for reader	❑	
Neat, easy to get the appropriate information	❑	
Subtotal	_____%	
Format		
Overall clarity	❑	
Slide organization	❑	
Appropriate amount of text on slides	❑	
Speed of presentation	❑	
Did all group members speak?	❑	
Total Summary Grade	_____%	

57. Group Project Progress Report

Week _____

Use this sheet (and attach any others needed) to record the progress that you and your group are making on the group project.

Completion status

0% _____ 50% _____ 100% literature review

0% _____ 50% _____ 100% introduction section

0% _____ 50% _____ 100% methodology

0% _____ 50% _____ 100% design

0% _____ 50% _____ 100% stimulus generation

0% _____ 50% _____ 100% data collection

0% _____ 50% _____ 100% method section

0% _____ 50% _____ 100% data analysis

0% _____ 50% _____ 100% data interpretation

0% _____ 50% _____ 100% poster/oral presentation

Summary of group progress this week (both inside and outside of the lab class):

Questions/issues that need to be resolved:

Things-to-do list:

Week _____

Use this sheet (and attach any others needed) to record the progress that you and your group are making on the group project.

Completion status

0% _____ 50% _____ 100% literature review

0% _____ 50% _____ 100% introduction section

0% _____ 50% _____ 100% methodology

0% _____ 50% _____ 100% design

0% _____ 50% _____ 100% stimulus generation

0% _____ 50% _____ 100% data collection

0% _____ 50% _____ 100% method section

0% _____ 50% _____ 100% data analysis

0% _____ 50% _____ 100% data interpretation

0% _____ 50% _____ 100% poster/oral presentation

Summary of group progress this week (both inside and outside of the lab class):

Questions/issues that need to be resolved:

Things-to-do list:

Week _____

Use this sheet (and attach any others needed) to record the progress that you and your group are making on the group project.

Completion status

0% _____ 50% _____ 100% literature review

0% _____ 50% _____ 100% introduction section

0% _____ 50% _____ 100% methodology

0% _____ 50% _____ 100% design

0% _____ 50% _____ 100% stimulus generation

0% _____ 50% _____ 100% data collection

0% _____ 50% _____ 100% method section

0% _____ 50% _____ 100% data analysis

0% _____ 50% _____ 100% data interpretation

0% _____ 50% _____ 100% poster/oral presentation

Summary of group progress this week (both inside and outside of the lab class):

Questions/issues that need to be resolved:

Things-to-do list:

Week _____

Use this sheet (and attach any others needed) to record the progress that you and your group are making on the group project.

Completion status
0% _____ 50% _____ 100% literature review
0% _____ 50% _____ 100% introduction section
0% _____ 50% _____ 100% methodology
0% _____ 50% _____ 100% design
0% _____ 50% _____ 100% stimulus generation
0% _____ 50% _____ 100% data collection
0% _____ 50% _____ 100% method section
0% _____ 50% _____ 100% data analysis
0% _____ 50% _____ 100% data interpretation
0% _____ 50% _____ 100% poster/oral presentation

Summary of group progress this week (both inside and outside of the lab class):

Questions/issues that need to be resolved:

Things-to-do list:

PART III

APA Style Exercises

The third component includes APA style exercises that begin with simple APA guidelines and progress to evaluation of short articles for APA style violations.
   (Exercises can be completed with any text chapter, depending on instructor preference for timing of APA style instruction.)

58. Sample APA Paper

Introduction to APA Publication

Style for Research Reports in Psychology

Dawn M. McBride

Illinois State University

Note: This sample paper adheres to the sixth edition of the *APA Publication Manual.*

Abstract

The purpose of this paper is to describe and model APA style of writing for research reports. Each section of an APA-style paper is described and is written according to the APA style guidelines to allow you to use it as a model. The Abstract summarizes the main points of the paper in 120 or fewer words. The Introduction should describe the research topic and hypotheses and the support for these hypotheses. The Method is written in subsections: Participants, Design, Materials, and Procedure. The study should be described in enough detail to replicate it. The Results section describes the data and any statistical tests used. The Discussion restates the hypotheses, giving evidence if they are supported.

Introduction to APA Publication
Style for Research Reports in Psychology

The purpose of the Introduction is to (a) describe the purpose of the study, (b) place the study in the context of previous research on the topic, and (c) justify your hypotheses (Smith, 2006). Each paragraph of the Introduction should bring the reader closer to understanding why the study was done and what hypotheses you are making.

The first paragraph of the Introduction should introduce the general topic of the study. Do not begin too generally (e.g., discussing all of psychology), but do not begin too specifically either (e.g., by stating the hypothesis). Be sure to define any terms you are using that are specific to the field of study. Indicate what your operational definitions are.

In subsequent paragraphs, you should be building a case for your study. Explain what has been found in previous research on this topic, describe what gap exists in this literature, and explain how your study will fill the gap (i.e., provide a unique study that will contribute new knowledge in the area).

Toward the end of your Introduction, you should briefly describe the design of your study in such a way that it connects to the justification you've given for the purpose of the study and leads to your hypotheses. Be sure to briefly review the justification for your hypotheses. Do not simply state your hypotheses and assume the reader will know why you are making them.

Method

In the Method section, you should describe the details of how the study was conducted. You should provide the reader with enough information to be able to replicate your study. Details that are not important for replication should not be included (e.g., what type of pencils the participants used). The reader should also be able to evaluate the appropriateness of your methods for the hypothesis you made. Method sections may vary in the number of sections the authors include, but the most common sections are described below. The entire Method section should be written in past verb tense.

APA STYLE FOR RESEARCH REPORTS   4

Participants

Describe who participated in your study. How many participants were in the study and how were they selected/recruited? In what way were the participants compensated for running in the study? Were any data sets deleted? If so, why were they deleted? Describe any demographics of the participants that were important to the study. If you've conducted an experiment, indicate how many participants were assigned to each condition.

Design

The design may appear separately in a journal article, or it may be combined with another section (e.g., Materials section). Either way, it is important to explain the design of the study. What variables were manipulated and/or measured? How were they manipulated/measured? If there are independent variables in the study, indicate the levels of each variable and whether each variable was manipulated within- or between-subjects.

Materials

Describe the materials used in the study. What were the stimuli? How were they developed? If appropriate, provide examples of the stimuli. Provide citations if the stimuli have been used in previous research. If there are questionnaires or surveys, describe them and relevant reliability and validity statistics.

Procedure

Describe the procedure of the study in chronological order. Explain what the participants did in the order they did them. Summarize the instructions. What tasks did they perform? In what order did they perform them? If different participants were exposed to different conditions, explain the differences in the conditions.

APA STYLE FOR RESEARCH REPORTS   5

Results

You should begin your Results section with a statement of your dependent measure. In addition, in your results section, you should describe the analysis conducted on your data. Also report the outcome of the analyses (e.g., means, standard deviations, *t* values, *F* values). Know the correct format for reporting statistics. Tables and Figures may accompany your Results section. Use tables or figures when they more clearly display results. Never include the same data in both a table and a figure (McBride & Wagman, 1997).

Discussion

The first part of your Discussion should review the hypotheses you stated in the Introduction, and you should state which hypotheses were supported by the data. State which results provided the support for a particular hypothesis.

In the second part of the Discussion section, you should compare your results to past studies, particularly studies discussed in the Introduction. If the results are not the same, discuss possible reasons for the difference.

Lastly, in your Discussion section, you should discuss the validity of your study. Were there any possible confounding variables that could have affected your results? If so, what were they and how did they specifically affect your data? You may also want to propose future research.

The Discussion section is less rigid than the other sections in format. You have more freedom here to discuss any relevant issues pertaining to your study. Be sure to end your Discussion section with a paragraph summarizing the contribution of your study. See the Appendix for some additional APA style writing tips.

References

McBride, D. M., & Wagman, J. B. (1997). Rules for reporting statistics in papers. *Journal of APA Style Rules, 105,* 55–67.

Smith, K. C. (2006). How to write an APA style paper in psychology. *Journal of APA Style Rules, 114,* 23–34.

APA STYLE FOR RESEARCH REPORTS   7

Appendix

Additional APA Style Writing Tips

---

8 1/2 × 11-inch good-quality paper

Use 1-inch margins

All text double-spaced

Start References on new page

No low-resolution printers

No handwritten corrections

Indent paragraphs five letter spaces (this can be more than five space bar strikes on a word-processing program)

No hyphenated broken words

Left margin justification for body of text

Do not right justify—leave right margin ragged

Number all pages except figures in upper right margin with short title (see Appendix)

Don't forget to include a Running Head on the Title Page

Include a separate page for figure captions

Correctly present numbers, including statistical copy

Use the metric system for all measurements

Use past tense to describe aspects of the study

Avoid sexist language

Spell check your work

Maintain correct subject–verb agreement

Do not underline words (italicize them)

Know the proper procedure for citations

Carefully reference every work used in your paper

59. Creating References

For the PsycINFO references listed below, rewrite each one in APA style.

1. Voss, Joel L; Paller, Ken A. Neural correlates of conceptual implicit memory and their contamination of putative neural correlates of explicit memory. [References]. [Journal; Peer Reviewed Journal] *Learning & Memory. Vol 14(1-6) Jan-Jun 2007, 259–267.* Year of Publication 2007

2. Carnagey, Nicholas L; Anderson, Craig A; Bushman, Brad J. The effect of video game violence on physiological desensitization to real-life violence. [References]. [Journal; Peer Reviewed Journal] *Journal of Experimental Social Psychology. Vol 43(3) May 2007, 489–496.* Year of Publication 2007

3. Blass, Thomas. Understanding behavior in the Milgram obedience experiment: The role of personality, situations, and their interactions. [References]. [Journal; Peer Reviewed Journal] *Journal of Personality and Social Psychology. Vol 60(3) Mar 1991, 398–413.* Year of Publication 1991

4. Wagman, Jeffrey B; Malek, Eric A. Perception of Whether an Object Can Be Carried Through an Aperture Depends on Anticipated Speed. [References]. [Journal; Peer Reviewed Journal] *Experimental Psychology. Vol 54(1) 2007, 54–61.* Year of Publication 2007

5. Meyers, Adena B; Landau, Steven. Best Practices in School-Based Sexuality Education and Pregnancy Prevention. [References]. [Book; Edited Book] *Thomas, Alex (Ed); Grimes, Jeff (Ed). (2002). Best practices in school psychology IV (Vol. 1, Vol. 2). (pp. 1523–1536). xv, 909 pp. Washington, DC, US: National Association of School Psychologists.* Year of Publication 2002

6. McDaniel, Mark A; Einstein, Gilles O. Spontaneous Retrieval in Prospective Memory. [References]. [Book; Edited Book] Nairne, James S (Ed). (2007). The foundations of remembering: Essays in honor of Henry L. Roediger, III. (pp. 225–240). xi, 451 pp. New York, NY, US: Psychology Press. Year of Publication 2007

60. APA Style Quiz

Choose the correct answer for each question that is consistent with APA style guidelines.

1. From the choices below, please choose the option that is correctly formatted in APA style:

    a. Neath, I., & Crowder, R. G. (1996). Distinctiveness and Very Short-term Serial Position Effects. *Memory, 4,* 225–242.

    b. Neath, Ian, & Crowder, Robert G. (1996). Distinctiveness and very short-term serial position effects. *Memory, 4,* 225–242.

    c. Neath, I., & Crowder, R. G. (1996). Distinctiveness and very short-term serial position effects. *Memory, 4,* 225–242.

    d. Neath, I., & Crowder, R. G. (1996), Distinctiveness and very short-term serial position effects, *Memory, 4,* 225–242.

2. From the choices below, please choose the option that is correctly formatted in APA-style:

    a. 12 subjects participated in the study.

    b. 12 participants volunteered for the study.

    c. 12 subjects participated in the study.

    d. Twelve participants volunteered for the study.

3. Choose the option below that indicates the correct ordering of headings in an APA-style paper:

    a. Participants, Method, Results, Procedure

    b. Method, Results, Participants, Procedure

    c. Method, Participants, Procedure, Results

    d. Results, Method, Participants, Procedure

4. Which of the following abbreviations should be used in an APA-style paper and do not need to be defined (choose all that apply)?

    a. *M* (for mean)

    b. IV (for independent variable)

    c. s (for seconds)

    d. *SD* (for standard deviation)

5. Which of the following is correct formatting for APA-style papers?

    a. single-spacing of text

    b. 1.5-inch margins

    c. begin References on a new page

    d. Abstract centered on title page

6. In what section of an APA-style paper would you find a reference to a table or figure?

    a. Introduction

    b. Method

    c. References

    d. Results

7. Which of the following is correct citation formatting?

    a. Talmi, Grady, Goshen-Gottstein, and Moscovitch (2005) reported that...

    b. Talmi and others in 2005 reported that...

    c. Talmi, 2005, reported that...

    d. In 2005, some researchers reported that...

8. Which of the following is NOT appropriate formatting for figures in an APA-style paper?

    a. figure title on the same page as the figure

    b. each figure on its own page

    c. figures at the end of the paper

    d. including a reference to the figures in the text

    e. none of the above

9. Which of the following does NOT belong on the title page?

    a. title of the paper

    b. running head

    c. Abstract

    d. authors' affiliations

10. An APA-style paper should be written in _____ verb tense.

    a. present

    b. past

    c. future

    d. conditional

61. APA Style Exercise

Identify as many APA style errors as you can find in the short paper below.

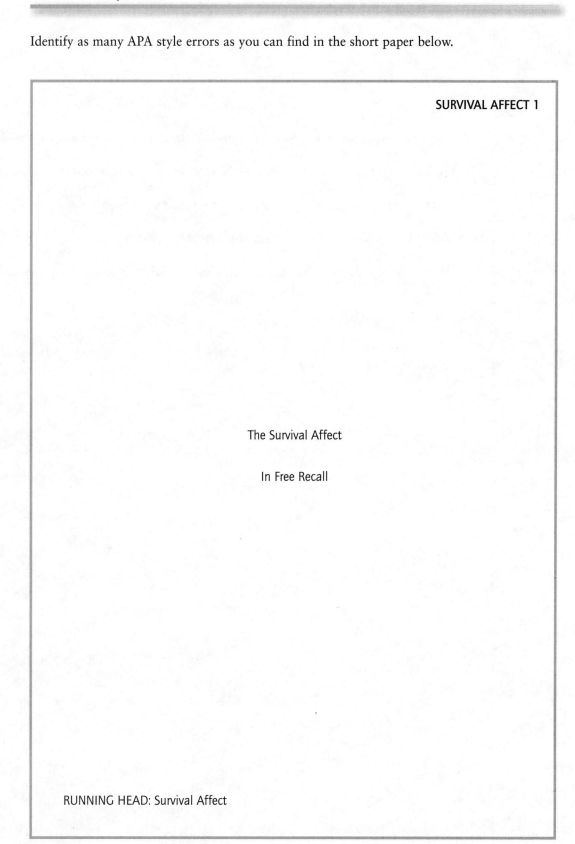

SURVIVAL AFFECT 1

The Survival Affect

In Free Recall

RUNNING HEAD: Survival Affect

Abstract

Memory for words studied in three different contexts was examined. In one study context, subjects rated items for their importance in surviving in the wilderness. In another context, subjects rated items for their importance in moving to another country. Finally, in the 3rd context, subjects rated the pleasantness of a list of items. Subjects then recalled the items in the list. Subjects were tested individually in a small lab room that measured 8 feet by 11 feet. Free recall results were very significant. Thus, the authors concluded that the survival affect is real. Further experiments confirmed this.

Introduction

We tested whether items studied in a survival context are better remembered than items studied in other contexts. Previous studies (like Nairne et al., 2007) have suggested that a survival context can improve memory. These results support the proposal that memory developed to aid human survival. The current study tested this.

Method

Subjects

Students from a psychology course volunteered. There were twenty-three of them. It was for course credit. Three came on a Monday and the rest came on a Thursday. Some were assigned to each context condition.

Materials

The experiment occurred in a small lab room with white walls. The floor had gray carpeting.

Subjects were tested individually in front of a computer. The experimenter told the subject that they would be rating items presented on the screen and then the instructions for one of the study contexts (survival, moving, pleasantness) were presented on the screen.

The items presented came from a norming study conducted in 2004 (Van Overschelde, Rawson, & Dunlosky). Each participant saw 44 items and rated each one according to the instructions. After the rating task, subjects were given a blank sheet of paper (8.5 inches by 11 inches) and asked to write down as many of the items as they remembered.

Procedure

Most of the procedure is described above. Items were presented for 4 seconds each in the rating task. Subjects were given 2 minutes to recall all the items in the list.

Results

Table 1. The results were very significant. A statistical test showed that F was 6.78. This was a p less than. 05 so our hypothesis was right. The means were 60% for survival, 52% for moving, and 53% for pleasantness. This shows that memory is important for survival.

Discussion

The experiment was designed well. We know this because our results showed significance. This tells us that experiencing things in a survival context can help our memory. This further proves that the purpose of memory is to help us survive. Future experiments can help prove this as well.

Table 1 Mean Percentage of Items Recalled as a Function of Study Context

Study Context	Mean
Survival	60
Moving	52
Pleasantness	53

References

James S. Nairne, Sarah R, Thompson, and Josefa N. S. Pandeirada, (2007). Adaptive Memory: Survival Processing Enhances Retention. *Journal of Experimental Psychology: Learning, Memory and Cognition*, Volume 33, No. 2, pgs. 263–273.

62. Sample Manuscript Text

HOMOPHONES 1

Where did Cinderella lose her slipper? At the dance or the soccer field: Homophones in language production

Windsor J. Page

Midwestern University

Mary A. Weaver

Midwestern University

One of the major problems that language users must deal with is the resolution of ambiguities. Consider the following examples:

a. Be alert! Your country needs alerts!

b. The cop saw the spy with the binoculars.

c. The man was not surprised when he inspected the bill.

In (a) the pun arises from the fundamental ambiguity that exists in the sounds of language. In spoken speech there are few acoustic cues to signal the beginning and ending of words. Thus "alert" can be parsed in a number of ways, two of which are "alert" and "a lert." In (b) there are two interpretations depending on the underlying grammatical structure: the cop had the binoculars or the spy had the binoculars. Finally, in (c) the ambiguity lies in the use of the homophone "bill," which could refer to an itemized list of costs or to the mouth of a duck. The experiments presented here were designed to explore the nature of lexical ambiguity (as in the third example), focusing primarily on the production processes.

Figure 1 presents a simplified model of the mental lexicon. The different levels of nodes represent different aspects of the words (sounds at the bottom, grammatical properties in the middle, and meanings in the cloud bubbles). During language comprehension and production, information flows up and down this network of nodes. Note that the model assumes that a homophone like "bill" has separate grammatical nodes, but share a single sound node.

The problem of lexical ambiguity has been widely studied in language comprehension (e.g. Swinney, 1979). One of the major questions of interest has focused on the role of context in ambiguity resolution. In general, the evidence suggests that when an ambiguous word (e.g., a homophone like "bill") is encountered all of its meanings (e.g., list of costs, duck beak, draft of proposed law, a short name for William) are initially activated and then the inappropriate meanings (as determined by the context) are quickly suppressed. However, some researchers have proposed that prior context can constrain the initial access, such that only the contextually appropriate meanings are activated (Tabbossi &Zardon, 1993).

The strategy of initial activation of multiple meanings followed by quick suppression of the inappropriate meanings is a sensible one for language comprehension since the nature of comprehension is to interpret potentially ambiguous input. The story is somewhat different for production because the producer faces a very different task than the comprehender. The producer knows the idea to be conveyed and must select the correct form to convey this meaning, thus the ambiguity that the producer faces does not reside at the level of interpretation or meaning. With respect to homophones, an initial activation of multiple meanings of a lexical item does not seem a useful strategy. Suppose that someone asked the question, "What is the beak of a duck called?" If the person answering the question selects the word bill to convey the idea of [the beak of a duck], it seems unlikely that he/she would also wish to activate the alternative meaning of bill (a list of fees). The fact that the lexical instantiation of the two meanings are phonologically identical should be irrelevant.

A current debate in language production research focuses on how information flows through the nodes. In the top-down modular approach (Levelt, 1989), activation flow is one-way, from the meaning level down to the sound level. A model that assumes this approach predicts that the alternative inappropriate meanings of a homophone (e.g., money when the duck meaning of bill is intended) should not receive any activation during the course of production. Alternatively, interactive theories propose that (e.g. Dell, 1986, 1990) information flow through the network is bidirectional (i.e., activation flows down and up the connections). This allows feedback from lower levels, to influence activation levels at higher levels. Models of this sort predict the activation of the alternative meaning of a homophone through feedback from the shared sound node.

The experiment presented here was designed to examine the issue of feedback in language production. We presented participants with simple questions during which an interfering word sometimes appeared on the screen. Their task was to answer the question as fast as they could after the offset of the question. For example, if the question was "At what event did Cinderella lose her slipper?," the participants were expected to answer "ball." There were three types of interfering words:

either a word related to the answer ("dance"), inappropriately related ("round," as in a toy ball) or a word unrelated to both meanings ("tree") to the answer of the question. The expectation was that the related words would exhibit an effect on the naming latencies to the questions relative to the unrelated words. The top-down modular view of production predicts that there should be no effect of the inappropriate interfering word. That is, the inappropriate condition should show the same pattern of results as the neutral condition. Additionally we manipulated the relative dominance of meaning for the homophones (e.g. the softball meaning of ball is more dominant than the dance meaning of ball).

Method Participants

Thirty-six Midwestern University students participated as part of a requirement in introductory psychology classes or for payment. All were native speakers of English.

Materials and Design

Twenty-four critical questions were created in such a way as to put much of the information near the end in an effort to prevent participants from coming up with the answer before the question's offset. In addition to the experimental items, we constructed and recorded forty-eight filler questions. These questions were designed to elicit simple one-word answers and were constructed to have a similar range of difficulty and level of informational content as the critical items. We constructed unrelated distracter words for twelve of these filler questions, so that the critical items would not be the only items with distracter words.

Using these items we constructed three lists each containing seventy-two questions. Within each of these lists, we manipulated the relatedness of the distracter word for each question, such that on each list one-third of the critical questions had appropriately related distracter words, one third inappropriately related distracter words, and the remaining third had unrelated distracter words.

Procedure

Participants were run in individual sessions. An example of a single trial was as follows. The participant initiated each trial by pressing the space bar on a computer. Through headphones, participants were presented a simple question. After the offset of the question, a question mark appeared (just above the center of the screen so that it would not interfere with distracter word) prompting the participant to answer the question aloud as quickly as possible. If the participant responded before the presentation of the question mark, then the computer terminated the question and signaled the participant that he had responded too quickly. During the critical questions (and a few filler questions) a distracter word was visually presented in the center of the screen for 1 second. Participants were instructed to try to read this word, but to try not to let it influence their answer to the question. Answering latencies and responses were recorded.

Results

The answering latencies for correct responses (answering the question using the target homophone) were examined using a within-group Analysis-of-variance. The ANOVA yielded a significant main effect of relatedness ($F(2, 34) = 14.4$, $p < 0.05$). Participants answered the questions most quickly with unrelated distracter words (630 msec). Distracters related to the appropriate meaning of the answer resulted in the slower answering latencies (720 msec) compared to those related to the inappropriate meaning (682 msec). These results are presented in Figure 2.

Discussion

The results of the experiment demonstrate that the presence of distracter words that were related (in meaning) to the question answer, slowed participants responses to the questions. This effect was strongest for words related to the appropriate meaning of the homophone answer (e.g., "beak" for the duck bill question). However, inappropriately related words (e.g., "money" for the duck bill question) also slowed answering latencies relative to unrelated distracters (e.g., "tree"). These results support the interactive approaches to language production.

References

Swinney, D. A. (1979). Lexical access during sentence comprehension: (Re)Consideration of context effects. *Journal of Verbal Learning and Verbal Behavior, 18,* 645–659.

Tabbossi, P. & Zardon, F. (1993). Processing ambiguous words in context. *Journal of Memory and Language,* 32, 359–372.

Levelt, W. J. M. (1989). *Speaking: From intention to articulation.* Cambridge, MA: MIT Press.

Dell, G. S. (1986). A spreading activation theory of retrieval in language production. *Psychological Review,* 93,283–321.

Dell, G. S. (1990). Effects of frequency and vocabulary type on phonological speech errors. *Language and Cognitive Processes,* 5, 313–349.

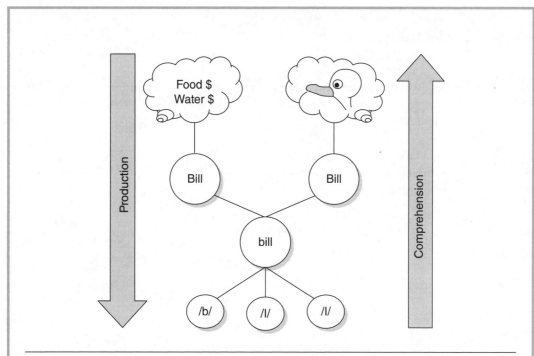

Figure 1 A simplified model of the language processing system.

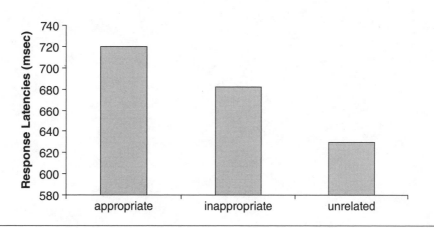

Figure 2 Answering latencies for experiment.

63. APA Exercise: Organizing and Formatting a Complete Report—Part A

The following assignment uses the sample manuscript text on pp. 105–108 (Where did Cinderella lose her slipper?). Your assignment is to reformat the text according to the following aspects of APA style.

- Double-space everything
- Set margins at 1 inch on all sides
- Create a title page, including all of the parts

64. APA Exercise: Organizing and Formatting a Complete Report—Part B

The following assignment uses the sample manuscript text (Where did Cinderella lose her slipper?). Your assignment is to reformat the text according to the following aspects of APA style. Use your completed *APA Exercise: Organizing and Formatting a Complete Report—Part A* as your starting place.

- Write an abstract

65. APA Exercise: Organizing and Formatting a Complete Report—Part C

The following assignment uses the sample manuscript text (Where did Cinderella lose her slipper?). Your assignment is to reformat the text according to the following aspects of APA style. Use your completed *APA Exercise: Organizing and Formatting a Complete Report—Part B* as your starting place.

- Format the headings and subheadings
- Insert a page header and page numbers
- Position the figures and figure caption pages appropriately

66. APA Exercise: Organizing and Formatting a Complete Report—Part D

The following assignment uses the sample manuscript text (Where did Cinderella lose her slipper?). Your assignment is to reformat the text according to the following aspects of APA style. Use your completed *APA Exercise: Organizing and Formatting a Complete Report—Part C* as your starting place.

- Order and correctly format the reference section
- Format all abbreviations and numbers according to APA guidelines
- Format all citations according to APA guidelines

67. APA Style Manuscript Checklist

Title Page

- ☐ Title
- ☐ Author(s)
- ☐ Affiliation(s)

Abstract

- ☐ Statement of the issue
- ☐ Brief hypothesis
- ☐ Brief description of the method
- ☐ Brief description of the results and conclusions

Introduction

- ☐ Problem of interest
- ☐ Link between problem and past research
- ☐ Summarize the past research
- ☐ Describe the basic purpose of the current experiment
- ☐ Describe hypotheses (conceptual level IV and DV)

Method

- ☐ Thoroughness of the description
- ☐ Participant description
- ☐ Design—IVs and DVs, operational definitions
- ☐ Materials—description of the stimuli
- ☐ Procedure—how the experiment was performed

Results

- ☐ Descriptive statistics
- ☐ What inferential statistics were used, what alpha level
- ☐ Results of the statistical analyses

Discussion

- ☐ Were the hypotheses supported or rejected?
- ☐ What are the implications of the results?
- ☐ Discussion of possible alternative explanations
- ☐ Future directions

References

- ☐ Are all the appropriate references cited?
- ☐ Are all the references cited in the text?
- ☐ Are the citations in the appropriate APA format?

Tables and Figures

- ☐ Figure captions page
- ☐ Each figure on a separate page
- ☐ Figures are clear/neat
- ☐ Tables follow APA style guidelines
- ☐ Tables and figures cited in text

Writing

- ☐ Overall clarity
- ☐ Grammar
- ☐ Spelling
- ☐ APA format

68. APA Style 6th Edition Update—A Summary of the Changes

The following table summarizes the style changes in APA with the publication of the sixth edition:

Section	Changes
Title Page	• Author note: includes (1) authors' names and affiliations, (2) changes of affiliation after the study was completed, (3) acknowledgments (individuals who aided in the completion of the study or the article, funding sources), (3) contact information for corresponding author. • Short title in header has been eliminated. • Running head: now appears at the top of every page, beginning with the title page.
Headers	• Headers are now bolded through the fourth header level. No headers are to be underlined.
Method	• Participants (Subjects) and Procedure subsections should be included, but other subsections may also be included or combined with the Procedure subsection.
Participants	• Use specific language to describe the study sample, such as college students, survey respondents, or children between the ages of 6 and 9 years. Terms such as *subjects* and *participants* are also allowed.
References	• Digital Object Identifiers (DOI) codes are now included with all sources that have them (primarily journal articles). The DOI code appears in the header or footer of the published article or in the full reference of the article in PsycINFO. The DOI is typed after the page numbers at the end of the reference. • References with more than seven authors should include the first six authors, an ellipsis (…), and the last author. • Consult the APA publication manual (www.apastyle.org) for reference style of electronic sources (e.g., websites, podcasts).
Tables	• Effective presentation of the data to maximize clarity should be used. Double-spacing around headings is no longer needed.
Figures	• Figure captions now appear on the same page as the figures, single-spaced.

More specific guidelines for the sixth edition of the manual are available at www.apastyle.org.

PART IV

Avoiding Plagiarism Exercises

Finally, the manual includes explanations of and exercises on plagiarism to help students understand what is and isn't plagiarism and how to avoid it in their writing.

- Academic Honesty Guidelines—What Is (and Isn't) Plagiarism
- Examples of Plagiarism
- Identifying and Avoiding Plagiarism

69. Academic Honesty Guidelines—What Is (and Isn't) Plagiarism

The required work for this class includes group work assignments, summaries of published work, and written research papers that will require the use of background sources. Therefore, it is especially important that you understand the guidelines regarding academic honesty. Here are some guidelines as they apply to specific assignments in this course:

1. Some lab exercises will be completed within a group. Although the discussion and preparation for completion of an assignment may be done by the group as a whole, the written assignment is your responsibility and must be written by you in your own words.

2. When writing your journal article summary, it will be necessary to use some of the terms in the article. However, the assignment is a summary of the article to be written in your own words. Do not quote from the article (quotes do not "summarize") and *do not use more than five words in succession from the article* or you will be plagiarizing the authors. A good way to prepare to write a summary is to make notes in your own words as you read the article, and then write from your notes instead of from the article itself. Re-ordering words in a sentence someone else has written also constitutes plagiarism.

3. The APA-style papers will require you to cite background sources (this means to indicate the authors and year of publication in parentheses when you get info from a source—it doesn't mean you can copy word for word from a source). You may not use more than five words in succession written by someone else in your paper unless you identify this material as a direct quote (by using quotation marks), and for most assignments in this course, you will not be allowed to quote (see the assignment sheets). If you are simply discussing what others reported in their written reports (without quoting), you must cite the authors when you begin the discussion. More information about proper citation procedures will be given in class, but see the APA manual for proper formatting of citations.

70. Examples of Plagiarism

The paragraphs below provide examples of three commonly used forms of plagiarism. Read through each paragraph and the explanations of the plagiarism examples. Then rewrite the original paragraph in your own words without plagiarizing the paragraph.

Original Paragraph

Author: Dawn McBride, 2006.

A patient known only as H.M. suffers from a particular form of amnesia. At the age of 27, H.M. had surgery to decrease the symptoms of his epilepsy. During the surgery, an area near the center of his brain called the hippocampus was damaged. The hippocampus aids in the storage of new memories. When H.M. awoke from the surgery, he could remember facts about himself and episodes from his life before the surgery, but he could not remember new people he met or new facts about the world or himself. In other words, H.M. has anterograde amnesia; since his surgery, he has not been able to create new memories that last longer than a few minutes. His condition keeps him from living a normal life.

Verbatim Plagiarism

Amnesia is a medical condition that has been found to impair an individual's ability to remember information. There is more than one type of amnesia that can affect an individual. **A patient known only as H.M. suffers from a particular form of amnesia. At the age of 27, H.M. had surgery to decrease the symptoms of his epilepsy.** When the surgery was being performed, **an area near the center of his brain called the hippocampus was damaged. The hippocampus aids in the storage of new memories.** Upon awakening from the surgery, **he could remember facts about himself and episodes from his life before the surgery, but he could not remember new people he met or new facts about the world or himself. In other words, H.M. has anterograde amnesia; since his surgery he has not been able to create new memories that last longer than a few minutes.** This unfortunate affliction limits the daily activities that H.M. is capable of engaging in.

Comments

The words highlighted in **bold** were written exactly as they appeared in the original passage. This is considered plagiarism, as the author of the rewritten passage has made no attempts to use quotation marks to indicate that the words were not his or her own. In addition, the author provides no citation for the work from which this information was taken. Although the entire passage has not been lifted from the original work, the author is still required to provide quotation marks and a citation.

Lifting Selected Passages

Amnesia is a medical condition that has been found to impair an individual's ability to remember information. There is more than one type of amnesia that can affect an individual. A *patient known only as H.M.* was affected by *a particular form of amnesia.* The treatment that H.M. underwent *to decrease the symptoms of his epilepsy* involved extensive surgical procedures wherein a section of his brain was removed to reduce the erratic electrical brain activity that was causing the seizures. During the procedure, *an area near the center of his brain* was damaged beyond repair. As a result, H.M. was no longer able to form new memories. Although H.M. could not form new memories, he could still *remember facts about himself and episodes from his life before the surgery.* This type of amnesia is called anterograde amnesia. This condition has precluded H.M. *from living a normal life.*

Comments

The paragraph above displays the author's attempt to paraphrase the original passage while only lifting select passages from the original. This is still considered plagiarism as the author used *five or more words in a row* from the original passage in several places without providing a citation or quotation marks. This type of plagiarism can be avoided by using quotation marks around the lifted passages and providing citations or by paraphrasing the lifted passages using his or her own words and providing a citation of the source.

Paraphrasing the Structure of the Paragraph Without Citations

An individual who was known in the medical community as H.M. was diagnosed with a specific type of amnesia. In order to reduce the number of seizures H.M. experienced as a result of his epilepsy, he underwent brain surgery when he was 27. When surgeons removed the afflicted areas of the brain, damage was caused to an area of the brain known as the hippocampus. Research has revealed that the primary function of the hippocampus is the formation of new memories. Upon awakening, H.M. found himself unable to store any new information regarding specific events and personal experiences. This type of amnesia is known as anterograde amnesia. H.M.'s memories that existed before the surgery remain preserved, whereas information encoded after the surgery is highly transient. This condition imposed severe limitations on the type and amount of daily activities that H.M. could complete without the assistance of others.

Comments

In this paragraph, the author did not lift any passages from the original paragraph. However, this paragraph has the same structure as the original and there are no citations. This is the most common type of plagiarism found. This type of plagiarism can be prevented by simply citing the source. For example, this paragraph could begin with a statement of who the original author was along with an indication that the following paragraph would be a restatement of the original author's words. In addition, the citation could come at the end of the paragraph if the author chooses.

71. Identifying and Avoiding Plagiarism

Consider the following abstract from:

Lane, L. W., Groisman, M., & Ferreira, V. S. (2006). Don't talk about pink elephants! Speakers' control over leaking private information during language production. *Psychological Science, 17,* 273–277.

Abstract

Speakers' descriptions sometimes inappropriately refer to information known only to them, thereby "leaking" knowledge of that private information. We evaluated whether speakers can explicitly control such leakage in light of its communicative consequences. Speakers described mutually known objects (e.g., a triangle) that had size-contrasting matches that were privileged to the speakers (e.g., a larger triangle visible to the speakers only), so that use of a contrasting adjective (e.g., small) involved referring to the privileged information. Half the time, speakers were instructed to conceal the identity of the privileged object. If speakers can control their leaked references to privileged information, this conceal instruction should make such references less likely. Surprisingly, the conceal instruction caused speakers to refer to privileged objects more than they did in the baseline condition. Thus, not only do speakers have difficulty not leaking privileged information, but attempts to avoid such leakage only make it more likely.

1. Write a summary of the abstract that uses three different kinds of plagiarism (as discussed in the "Examples of Plagiarism" above).

2. Rewrite your summary without using any plagiarism.

Appendix

Guide to Using Lab Manual Exercises With *The Process of Research in Psychology* (3rd Edition), by Dawn M. McBride

References

Assefi, S. L., & Garry, M. (2003). Absolut memory distortions: Alcohol placebos influence the misinformation effect. *Psychological Science, 14*, 77–80.

Bartecchi, C., Alsever, R. N., Nevin-Woods, C., Thomas, W. M., Estacio, R. O., Bartelson, B. B., & Krantz, M. J. (2006). Reduction in the incidence of acute myocardial infarction associated with a citywide smoking ordinance. *Circulation, 114*, 1490–1496.

Braun K. A., & Loftus, E. F. (1998). Advertising's misinformation effect. *Applied Cognitive Psychology, 12*, 569–591.

Cantlon, J. F., & Brannon, E. M. (2006). Shared system for ordering small and large numbers in monkeys and humans. *Psychological Science, 17*, 401–406.

Chartrand, T. L., & Bargh, J. A. (1999). The chameleon effect: The perception–behavior link and social interaction. *Journal of Personality and Social Psychology, 76*, 893–910.

Farmer, H., McKay, R., & Tsakiris, M. (2014). Trust in me: Trustworthy others are seen as more physically similar to the self. *Psychological Science, 25*, 290–292.

Farooqui, A. A., & Manly, T. (2015). Anticipatory control through associative learning of subliminal relations: Invisible may be better than visible. *Psychological Science, 26*, 325–334.

Ferreira, V. S., & Humphreys, K. R. (2001). Syntactic influences on lexical and morphological processing in language production. *Journal of Memory and Language, 44*, 52–80.

Jackson, J. J., Connolly, J. J., Garrison, S. M., Leveille, M. M., & Connolly, S. L. (2015). Your friends know how long you will live: A 75-year study of peer-rated personality traits. *Psychological Science, 26*, 335–340.

Jirout, J. J., & Newcombe, N. S. (2015). Building blocks for developing spatial skills: Evidence from a large, representative U.S. sample. *Psychological Science, 26*, 302–310.

Jordan, J. S., & Knoblich, G. (2004). Spatial perception and control. *Psychonomic Bulletin & Review, 11*, 54–59.

Lane, L. W., Groisman, M., & Ferreira, V. S. (2006). Don't talk about pink elephants! Speakers' control over leaking private information during language production. *Psychological Science, 17*, 273–277.

Lawson, T. J. (2007). *Readings in pseudoscience and the paranormal*. Upper Saddle River, NJ: Pearson.

Lee, K., Talwar, V., McCarthy, A., Ross, I., Evans, A., & Arruda, C. (2014). Can classic moral stories promote honesty in children? *Psychological Science, 25*, 1630–1636.

Logan, G. D. (2004). Working memory, task switching, and executive control in the task span procedure. *Journal of Experimental Psychology: General, 133*, 218–236.

Mueller, P. A., & Oppenheimer, D. M. (2014). The pen is mightier than the keyboard: Advantages of longhand over laptop notetaking. *Psychological Science, 25*, 1159–1168.

Nauta, M. M. (2007). Assessing college students' satisfaction with their academic majors. *Journal of Career Assessment, 15*, 446–462.

Plomin, R., Fulker, D. W., Corley, R., & DeFries, J. C. (1997). Nature, nurture, and cognitive development from 1 to 16 years: A parent-offspring adoption study. *Psychological Science, 8*, 442–447.

Roediger, H. L., III, & Karpicke, J. D. (2006). Test-enhanced learning: Taking memory tests improves long-term retention. *Psychological Science, 17*, 249–255.

Sayette, M. A., Reichle, E. D., & Schooler, J. W. (2009). Lost in the sauce: The effects of alcohol on mind wandering. *Psychological Science, 20*, 747–752.

Sproesser, G., Schupp, H. T., & Renner, B. (2014). The bright side of stress-induced eating: Eating more when stressed but less when pleased. *Psychological Science, 25*, 58–65.

Tsapelas, I., Aron, A., & Orbuch, T. (2009). Marital boredom now predicts less satisfaction 9 years later. *Psychological Science, 20*, 543–545.

Vohs, K. D., & Schooler, J. W. (2008). The value of believing in free will. *Psychological Science, 19*, 49–54.

Index of Concepts
and Terms

Notes

Notes